JUDO

JUDO

History, Theory, Practice

Vladimir Putin
Vasily Shestakov &
Alexey Levitsky

North Atlantic Books
Berkeley, California

Published by   Cover and book design by Brad Greene
North Atlantic Books   Printed in the United States
P.O. Box 12327   Distributed to the book trade
Berkeley, California 94712   by Publishers Group West
Originally printed in Russian by Neva Olma Press

Translation and publication made possible by a grant from George F. Russell, Jr.

Judo: History, Theory, Practice is sponsored by the Society for the Study of
Native Arts and Sciences, a nonprofit educational corporation whose goals
are to develop an educational and crosscultural perspective linking various
scientific, social, and artistic fields; to nurture a holistic view of arts, sciences, humanities, and healing; and to publish and distribute literature on
the relationship of mind, body, and nature.

North Atlantic Books' publications are available through most bookstores.
For further information, call 800-337-2665 or visit our website at
www.northatlanticbooks.com.

Substantial discounts on bulk quantities are available to corporations, professional associations, and other organizations. For details and discount
information, contact our special sales department.

Library of Congress Cataloging-in-Publication Data

Putin, Vladimir Vladimirovich, 1952-
    [Uchimsëiìa dzëiìudo s Vladimirom Putinym. English]
    Judo : history, theory, practice / by Vladimir Putin, Vasily Shestakov,
and Alexey Levitsky.
       p. cm.
    ISBN 1-55643-445-6 (pbk.)
    1. Judo. I. Shestakov, Vasiliæi. II. Leviëtìskiæi, Alekseæi. III. Title.
    GV1114.P8613 2004
    796.815'2--dc22
                                                              2004007151
                                                                     CIP

1 2 3 4 5 6 7 8 9 DATA 09 08 07 06 05 04

Table of Contents

Preface

I am honored to present this work by Vladimir Putin and his associates. Whatever else English-speaking people may know about the career of President Putin, they should realize that he is a judo master. His judo-based senses of discipline, honor, and service to humankind as President of the Russian Federation tower over any of the more menial roles assigned to him in the former Soviet Union. Insofar as judo is at his core, he brings a warrior's presence to the international stage. Judo may not be the answer to the economic woes of Russia, but it does have broad impact on the philosophy of those who practice it. As a sport that demands mental sobriety and physical endurance and encompasses intellectual and physical discipline, it helps focus the minds and bodies of people in a country that is undergoing radical change, while contributing to their better health. In particular, judo emphasizes concentration, self-determination, poise, and inner strength.

Created as the "gentle art" by founder Jigiro Kano, judo is known throughout the world as a sport that puts near total emphasis on the development of character. Master Kano saw judo as a way for the physically inferior practitioner to rely on inner strength and force of will to defeat a larger, more aggressive foe. In the weighty arena of global politics, discipline and quiet self-confidence are crucial attributes in successfully guiding national policies. History shows that the bully who relies on brute force and overwhelming firepower always falls to another empire mightier still. The maturity and poise born of judo practice is an unfailing guide in such matters. Judo elicits balance and collaboration, albeit a wary détente among centers of power. By relying on the clarity and determination ingrained through the dedicated forging of one's spirit in the dojo, a judoka is always in the position to identify his opponent's weakness and bring about a "gentle" victory. In the realm of world understanding, the principles of judo thus suggests a world community in the future in which global cooperation and exchange among nations can take the place of reliance on weaponry and threats. In a judo-oriented realm of politics, the true inner creativity and capacity of the human species may be realized.

A book on judo in English could be a book repeating many others in times past. But a book written by President Putin has a chance to awaken the English-speaking world to a person who is totally devoted to bringing the new Russia successfully into the global market place as a competitive and peaceful competitor. And believe me, President Putin, as a judo expert, understands what competition is all about! I believe this book can be a catalyst to promote international understanding of the new Russia's dynamic leader.

I am pleased to play a role in not only bringing President Putin's message to the English speaking world, but also to help Russia on its difficult road to become an economic competitor on the world stage.

I was the original financial supporter in 1994 of "Kukly" on Russian television when the primary purpose of the muppet show was to explain free-market economics. When the show's focus switched to politics, I terminated my support. My goal is to work on matters that transcend regional politics. I am now funding scientific research by Russian scientists on how to destroy nuclear waste . . . and how to bury the residual.

Under the EastWest Institute (EWI) and its center in Moscow, I initiated what we originally called the "Private Sector Marshall Plan." The name was later changed to the "Private Sector Initiative" (PSI). The key focus of PSI is now "The Kendall-Russell Centre for Corporate Competitiveness in Russia." Its purpose is to help break up logjams that keep the forces of a free market economy from becoming efficient and effective. An outsider has no real appreciation for the gridlock that exists in Russia today. The challenges of starting a new business in Russia, remind me of the same problem in Poland during their transition . . . 150 hurdles to jump in order to start a new business, a gauntlet was eventually reduced to one page! The need for unconditional transparency in the government as well as in the private sector is equally essential in Russia if the country is to become competitive in the world economy. Our mission is to break logjams like these and let market forces march forward.

The EastWest Institute is not a "think-tank" as much as it is a "do things on the ground tank." Martti Ahtisaari, the former President of Finland, and I presently co-chair this organization. One of its "on the ground" projects of fairly brief duration was played out in 2001 with President Putin and President Bush.

In 1988, before I was involved, the Institute brought in Senators David Boren, John Danforth, and Alan Simpson as Co-Chairs on how America should treat Mikhail Gorbachev. Their masterpiece of objective analysis got wide global recognition.

President Putin saw the report and suggested a similar scrutiny of himself. At that time, President Bush and President Putin were staring at each other without an encouraging look in their eyes. What we wanted was for them to start holding hands, figuratively speaking. We got the three Senators back together, they prepared the report, and on July 2, 2001, the three Senators, John Mroz the founder and President of EWI, and I met for about an hour with President Putin in the Kremlin. Three weeks later we were at the White House meeting with President Bush on the same matter. Ask any informed insider, and you will hear that that effort had a big effect on the way President Putin reacted after the tragedy on September 11, 2001, in the United States.

President Putin supports all of the major things that must be done to achieve his goal of effectively entering the world economic competition. His judo-like principles and behavior are behind all of this. He is convinced Russia will achieve his goals.

I also believe whole-heartedly in the global economy and free trade, if done right. These powerful forces have already lifted millions out of poverty. Since 1979 when Deng Xiao Ping decided to allow free trade for China, there has correspondingly been the largest reduction of poverty that the world has ever witnessed. I will take this a step further: without free trade, I believe poverty cannot be resolved. In my opinion, it is the only possible way to reduce the huge difference between the poor and the wealthy.

Somewhat myopically, unions in the United Sates tend to preach otherwise; they are afraid of losing job security. For example, many union members see that China is beginning to produce generators and that it may threaten some jobs in the United States. When there was a world event in Seattle a few years ago, Boeing's union took to the streets against globalization. What they did not realize was that their jobs depended on free trade because they sell many more airplanes overseas than they do in the United

States. Forces of cyclical differentiation and regional centralization are virtual laws of nature. They operate on a cultural level even as they influence stars, continents, weather, plant and animal populations. In truth, only a global approach can solve the complex environmental and economic problems the world now faces.

In three hundred years, we will have a single global currency. Some countries will be making steel; other countries will be growing cotton. In the United States, we now have 25,000 cotton producers and they are all wealthy because the United States Government pays them three and a half billion dollars a year, so they can afford to grow cotton and sell it below real market prices. No one who wants to grow cotton in Africa can plant fields and compete. If we had to do things the right way, is that the way to do them? Absolutely not! Now this planet has to begin to do things the right way because there is no future in the present version of inequity and inefficiency, especially as populations increase and non-sustainable resources are consumed. Globalization with free trade is a way that we can change our basic political and economic realities without violence. I expect President Putin shares this way of thinking.

Let me conclude by saying that it may be a new age of campaigning if President Putin makes good on his idea to do a judo demonstration at Madison Square Garden. We would fill Madison Square Garden if he offered to put his judo gear on and demonstrate his sport. This then would be the real thing—politician as martial artist, the martial artist as politician. No doubt, he would put some professional wrestlers and body-builders to shame, but then he would (equally no doubt) graciously allow himself to be thrown by a precocious American high-school judoka studying Master Kano's art.

George F. Russell, Jr.
Co-Chairman: EastWest Institute
Co-Chairman: The Kendall-Russell Centre for Corporate Competitiveness in Russia
Chairman: Transmutation Technologies, Inc.
Chairman: National Bureau of Asian Research
Chairman: The Russell Family Foundation
Honorary Co-Chairman: The Business Humanitarian Forum
Chairman Emeritus: Frank Russell Company

Introduction

I am very happy to see this wonderful book by Vladimir Putin, Vasily Shestakov, and Alexey Levitsky. It is rare and very inspiring that a head of state would make such an investment of time to write a book like this. It is a fine gift to the judokas of the world as well as to those of Russia.

The history of judo is very important. In researching and recording the many experiences of Kano Sensei as he developed judo, the authors remind us of the essential philosophical and spiritual components of judo that are too often forgotten. Kano Sensei was impressed by the integrity of his teachers, including my grandfather, Hachinosuke Fukuda, who was his first jujitsu instructor. Kano Sensei developed his skill and passed on this inspiration to his early students, even in the face of conflict around him, while developing codes of behavior and training that exemplified his mottos: "Mutual Welfare and Benefit" and "Best Use of Energy."

When Kano Sensei invited me to come to the Women's Section of the Kodokan in 1934, I began my lifelong commitment to judo. Within a few years, I knew that I could honor his request to help spread judo throughout the world by diligent practice and dedicated teaching. I began to travel and to teach in many countries while I studied his work more deeply, which led me to writing. Similarly, President Putin's book supports and confirms Kano Sensei's vision that judo be embraced and cultivated in all countries. In many ways, this book is an ambassador, furthering a common language among judo students and other martial artists. Besides offering a fascinating exploration of judo history, it includes theories and provides guidance for effective practice through healthy diet, exercise, and focused study. Specific details about proper breakfalls, throwing techniques, and matwork will help judokas at all levels, everywhere. And finally, the conclusion is not a conclusion at all, but rather an invitation, an open hand, to any and all women and men who might want to join us on the mat and learn this most invigorating martial art, judo, "the way of gentleness." Vladimir Putin Sensei and his co-writers have established themselves as gifted writers and contributors to the judo world.

Keiko Fukuda, 9th Dan, United States Judo Federation
San Francisco, California

A Look at the Past

The Beginning

Judo owes its origins to a centuries-old tradition of one-on-one military combat that came into being and developed in various schools of jujitsu in medieval Japan, yet many people still argue about whether jujitsu has purely Japanese roots or if it was brought in from outside. It is a delicate issue, as it touches on the Japanese patriotic feelings.

There are three versions of the story of jujitsu's origin. According to the first story, China is the homeland of jujitsu; jujitsu penetrated the Japanese islands when a monk named Chen Yuanbin arrived in the Land of the Flowering Sakura. Having left China due to the terror of the Ming dynasty, he found a refuge in one of the monasteries in Edo. He lived modestly, away from the noise and the hustle and bustle, taught Chinese calligraphy and philosophy to the children of noblemen, and translated classics of Chinese literature. He traveled occasionally, painting monotone landscapes, but most importantly he taught fighting techniques to many samurai warriors, which helped to spread jujitsu in Japan.

The second version of jujitsu's origin is connected with the name of Take-nouchi Hishamori, who, according to legend, dreamed of a hermit monk who came down from the mountains and shared the secrets of an art based on throwing and fighting techniques. Thus the purely national origin of jujitsu is established.

Finally, the story of Doctor Akayama Shirobei is widely known. He would often take walks in the garden in wintertime and admire the branches of a cherry tree (other sources say it was a spruce) that slept soundly in expectation of spring, tilting forward its cap of white snow. One time, Akayama noticed that one thick branch couldn't support the weight of the snow and had snapped. But a small, flexible branch was bent all the way to the ground, yet it didn't break. When Akayama saw this, he fell into contemplation and exclaimed, "You must first surrender in order to ultimately gain victory!" His words related to the fighting techniques that he was in the process of creating. Having studied the hand-to-hand combat systems known as *kogusoku* and *kosinomawari*, which were popular in Japan at that time, he set off for China in order to expand his knowledge. In China, he became familiar with a series of local fighting styles called *subak* and *taijitsuisho*. As a result of systematizing and generalizing technique, Akayama, along with his students and colleagues, demonstrated several thousand techniques to a specially convened imperial commission. These techniques formed the foundation of jujitsu.

German art historian and jujitsu expert Karl Hageman stated in the 1920s that the fighting style of jujitsu derives, like everything in Japan (for example, karate), from China. This generally correct statement (let's remember karate) should be made more precise, since these borrowings were usually subjected to a purely national reworking and reconceptualizing by the Japanese and acquired an independent character, often on a higher level.

As a term that generalizes and systematizes the experience of hand-to-hand contests on the battlefield, the word *jujitsu* appeared at the end of the fourteenth century. During the reign of the Tokugawa shogunate, a period of more than three hundred years during which martial arts flourished in Japan, the number of jujitsu schools approached seven hundred.

The latter half of the nineteenth century marked the beginning of an age of striking changes in Japan. In 1868, supported by advocates of radical reforms, the emperor Mutsuhito ascended the throne. The revolutionary transformations of the Meiji Restoration era began in all spheres of society. The country's prolonged period of isolation ended as the spirit of the West began to infiltrate the daily life of ordinary Japanese. A generation interested in everything new and modern stepped out onto the historical stage. European theater and rugby became symbols of this generation. The samurai tradition died off. The ancient martial arts, which were carried on by representatives of samurai clans, were threatened.

The speedy diffusion of Western cultural elements in Japanese society played a role in the appearance of judo as well. Jigoro Kano was the creator of this multifaceted system of physical education and art. He tied together the ideals of the samurai and the gentler side of jujitsu and called the result "judo," from *ju-,* meaning "the gentle way," and *-do,* which identifies the system as an art and a way of life, as well as a sport.

Kano was born on October 28, 1860, in the prefecture of Hyogo in the small town of Mikage, not far from Kyoto. On his father's side, Kano's roots trace back to the very beginning of Japanese history; among his ancestors are Shinto monks, Buddhist masters, and followers of Confucius. His mother, Sadako, traced her lineage to one of the most famous sake-producing clans. Kano had one brother and two sisters, and he was the youngest. From his earliest years Kano showed a proclivity for the humanities, demonstrating (as did the majority of Japanese children) diligence and tirelessness. When the boy turned eleven, the whole family moved to Tokyo, where the future patriarch of judo continued his studies at two institutions. At one he studied the complex Japanese system of calligraphy, and at the other he studied English. He started his modern education at thirteen, when his father, convinced of his son's talent, enrolled Kano in a private British school. There the young Kano soon rose to the top of his class but did not win over the physical education teachers. His school friends looked down on him, literally, since Kano had been a weakling since birth and, even by Japanese standards, was small in stature.

At that time, jujitsu was neither fashionable nor respected in Japan, let alone considered a worthy activity for young boys from decent families. Neither Kano's father nor his friends approved of his decision to find a jujitsu teacher, despite the fact that Kano, who had an unyielding character, could stand up for himself when fighting with the other boys, even later in his student years. By modern standards Kano began his training in martial arts rather late—at age seventeen—but this only confirms the idea that all ages succumb to the martial arts, just as they do to love.

At the same time, Kano entered Kaisei School, which later became Tokyo Imperial University, where he majored first in economics and then pedagogy.

During his studies, he met Takaaki Kato and Kumazo Tsuboi, a meeting that was to play an important role in the subsequent history of judo. One of his new friends would later become prime minister, the other the rector of Tokyo University Cultural Center, where European ideas and achievements were promoted. Japanese youth in the age of crisis enthusiastically discovered the hitherto banned culture of the West, developing a passion for its theater, boycotting Kabuki, and dressing according to European fashions. Unsurprisingly, in such an atmosphere, Kano's appeals to revert to Japanese fighting traditions were misunderstood among his university friends, whose gazes were turned toward the unknown and alluring European sports of cricket, rowing, and baseball.

The young man's search for jujitsu instruction led him to the school of Tenshin Shinyo, which had been revived by jujitsu master Mataemon Iso. Kano had received some instruction in basic technique from Teinosuke Yagi, who noticed his student's gifts and wrote a letter of introduction for him, which was required in order for the young man to be accepted by Hachi-nosuke Fukuda, the school's director and an authority in Eastern medicine. Here was a professional who knew his trade and who religiously preserved the secrets of the ancient martial art. According to Kano's memoirs, Fukuda was a most noble person and greatly sympathized with his young student. Fukuda used *randori*—a form of free practice—as the fundamental means for training in his classes. Following the teacher's demonstration of a given jujitsu technique, the student was required to strive to master the technique in practice matches. Kano trained doggedly and achieved great success. However, Kano's creative interaction with the old master was short-lived. Fukuda died in 1879, bequeathing to Jigoro Kano the notebooks that he had kept regarding the school.

During his studies under Sensei Fukuda, the young Kano would often meet with a certain Kanekichi Fukushima, who was twice as heavy as Kano. Fukushima—a fish wholesaler and the strongest and most experienced of Fukuda's students—often filled in for the master himself in training sessions when the master's health started failing him. Kano's repeated attempts to overcome his opponent's superior physical conditioning always ended in failure. Judo's future creator gave much thought to ways of beating this strong but awkward opponent.

One time, Kano came to class with a plan. He arrived for training earlier than usual, sat down in a corner, and observed the fighting style and movements of his potential opponent for a while. At the end of the workout, Kano changed clothes and, respectfully bowing to Fukushima, asked to spar with him. Fukushima burst out laughing and readily agreed. With many victories under his belt, he was certain of success. Kano stood 2 meters from his opponent, with no apparent intention of attacking. Somewhat disheartened and vexed, Fukushima took a step forward and, as he took his second step, grabbed the collar of Kano's *gi* (martial arts outfit) with lightning speed. That's exactly what Kano, who had set up and anticipated the situation, was waiting for. He grabbed the attacker's hand with his opposite hand, made a quarter turn toward Fukushima, and, bending his knees, shoved his opponent, who had lost his balance, with his other hand. Fukushima, under the deathly silence of the onlookers, fell on his back with a thud. The astonishment of the onlookers was intensified by the fact that the fallen opponent, stunned by the throw, was unable to get up for a long time.

This decisive victory gave judo's creator the chance to confirm that he was right about the importance of a set of techniques—like *kuzushi*—for putting an opponent off-balance in preparation for a throw. Any novice *judoka* (judo practitioner) knows that today. But at that time, for many people, the technique was a revelation. Jigoro Kano himself maintained that kuzushi was an important stage of a throw, since an opponent, even a more powerful one, can be overcome without too much effort after being properly off-balanced. After the death of Sensei Fukushima, who had given his young student the basics of jujitsu, Kano had to search for a new teacher.

Kano got lucky this time, too, although everyone knows that the strong are lucky and only those who seek shall find. His new teacher was Masamoto Iso, the third master of the Tenshin Shinyo school. At that time, Iso was already sixty-two. He was a frail, short man, who bore a physical resemblance to his new student. With his unusual personality, strength of character, and astounding mastery of jujitsu, Iso commanded the genuine respect of those around him. Later on, the patriarch of judo would give high marks to the training methods of Iso's school and believed that he had never met anyone so good at performing and demonstrating *kata* (set forms) as his sensei. Iso died two years later and, like Fukuda, left his notebooks to his student.

Fortunately, Jigoro Kano had good teachers from the very beginning. The first was a master fighter, and the second was a master at teaching technique. At the Tenshin Shinyo school, Kano received the rank of *shihan* (master); this was his most fruitful period. He rose early in the morning, often beginning his training at sunrise, and then went to classes at the university. From there he went back to the *dojo* (martial arts studio), where he would train a group of beginners. In 1881, after Iso had fallen ill, Jigoro Kano met Tsunetoshi Iikubo from the Kito school, which had been founded back in 1670 by Terada Kanemon, and changed jujitsu teachers for the third time. Iikubo was a former samurai and, for a long time, conducted jujitsu in the shogunate. When fate first brought Kano and Iikubo together, the master was still able to show Kano many things personally, having maintained, to put it in modern terms, a good athletic build. The ex-samurai lived in poverty and was faithful to jujitsu to the end of his life. Iikubo's new student not only learned elegance of movement from him, but also persistence and hardiness. Kano combined practice with a study of the manuscripts of this branch of jujitsu, and, just a year later, his teacher was forced to acknowledge: "I have nothing left to teach you."

Soon came a trial. The rector of Tokyo University was in the habit of inviting representatives from various sports to give demonstrations at the school, with the goal of promoting physical education to the youth. The next demonstration took place in the newly built large assembly hall, which held around a hundred people. This time students from a jujitsu school headed by an eighty-year-old teacher named Tozuka were invited.

At that time, there were no competition rules for jujitsu. Fighting could incorporate any kind of grabs, and the loser was the one who ended up on his back, conceded defeat, or was unable to continue fighting. There was no time limit for the matches. When the demo performances had ended, Master Tozuka asked all those present, "Would anyone like to spar?" Jigoro Kano could not pass up an opportunity to test himself and challenged the most powerful student. All attempts to overpower his tall and powerful opponent came to naught. His opponent not only possessed tremendous strength but also high-level fighting technique. Nonetheless, Jigoro Kano appeared to be the victor, for he earned the praise both of the university rector and of his disheartened master for his courage and ability. This meeting later encouraged Kano to continue his work in the martial arts.

Despite his intense classes at the university, Kano took advantage of every opportunity he could to train. In the summer of 1882, he received his degree as a literature teacher, which brought him closer to members of the intellectual elite of Japanese society. Kano decided to continue his education in a school of aristocrats, which would later open up a promising career in government service. But his passion for jujitsu, which had become his life, changed the course of his destiny.

In February of that year, Kano and several of his students opened their own school in Eishoji Temple in Tokyo. This was the now world-renowned Kodokan, which back then occupied four areas. The largest—an area of about 4 by 6 meters—was made into the dojo. In the school's first year, there were only ten students. The novice teacher didn't have enough money to equip even the smallest of the halls, so Kano obtained the needed sum by translating a book called *A Treatise on Ethics* by order of the ministry of education.

The date that Kodokan opened is considered to be the birth date of judo—an original system for educating Japanese youth, created by Jigoro Kano and based on ancient jujitsu—a system of physical and moral perfection that filled not only a practical function but an educational function and, more importantly, a character-building function as well. One of the major tenets of judo is perfection of human character through the on-going practice of the martial art, making it a lifelong study. The dojo led into the temple's main hall, where wooden tablets dedicated to the memory of the dead hung on the walls. Often, when the fighting was especially intense, the shaking of the floor caused the tablets to rattle. In the evening, this resembled a dance of mysterious spirits. In this unusual setting, the sounds of the falling plaques and, at times, the creaking of the broken floorboards, which could not withstand the stress of the falling bodies, caused the rare visitors to shudder. After the training sessions, the teacher himself, Kano, would crawl under the floor, wrapping his head in a towel so as to shield himself from the thick cobwebs, reinforce the beams, and replace the broken floorboards. The next day the whole process would repeat itself.

Kano divided his time between Buddhist training and research. The greater part of his day was spent with students at the temple, where he ate, sewed and repaired workout clothes, engaged in conversation, and conducted classes. At the same time, he found himself having to perform the functions of teacher at the renowned Gakushuin school, where the children of the privileged studied. Classes started early in the morning. Kano devoted the second half of the day to judo then took some notes and prepared his plan for the next day and translated foreign texts, sometimes working till well past midnight.

Many of those who knew Kano and visited his workouts were important figures in society. Several students came from aristocratic families. Surprised monks and residents of neighboring homes would often see the carriages of ministers parked by the doors of the temple. Despite the interest Kano's system received, it was obvious that the monks' long suffering would not be eternal. One time, the director of the temple came to the dojo and, observing the master and his students hard at work, remarked significantly, "Jigoro Kano is an outstanding person, despite his young age. His only shortcoming is his passion for judo." Twice, sometimes three times a day, Sensei Tsunetoshi Iikubo would come to the school. The matches could be extraordinarily intense at times, and, not surprisingly, eventually Jigoro Kano's students requested that a new place for training be found.

In January 1883, the Kodokan left Eishoji Temple and found a new refuge in a very modest location. The new hall could not accommodate all the tatami, so Kano made a small structure, which, although more spacious, did not protect from the cold and dampness. A year later, the master and his students, whose number had grown significantly, were relieved to find out about the opportunity to relocate to another hall. That year, Kano developed a code of conduct for the students of the Kodokan. The first ones to sign it, dipping their hands in their own blood, were Tsunejiro Tomita, Seiko Higuchi, Shiro Saigo, Sakujiro Yokoyama, and Yoshiaki Yamashita. The same day Shiro Saigo and Tsunejiro Tomita, the school's oldest students, received their black belts as a symbol of having achieved the first master degree.

Jigoro Kano established the five points of the oath, whose meaning can be summarized as follows:

- Upon embarking on the path of judo, I shall not refuse to train unless I have serious reasons for doing so.
- I promise not to demean the dignity of judo through my behavior.
- I shall never betray the secrets of the school to the uninitiated and only in extreme cases shall I take fighting lessons at another location.

- I promise not to give lessons without the permission of my sensei.
- Throughout my life I promise to respect the rules of the Kodokan, both as a student and teacher, if I become a teacher.

At first no one saw or understood the difference between jujitsu and judo. The old masters, without taking the time to delve into the essence of the ideas put forth by Jigoro Kano, considered him a nonsensical upstart who prided himself on his education and tried to introduce foreign Western ways into the national traditions of the ancient martial arts. After a time, sensing a threat from judo, the representatives of jujitsu declared a merciless fight against Kano. The final years of the nineteenth century turned out to be difficult ones for judo, which was coming into its own, had launched a struggle for the right of citizenship in the new Japan, and was soon to emerge as an integral element of the culture of the Land of the Rising Sun.

In their efforts to gain recognition, Kano's students had to prove the superiority of the new system in practice. Soon after the first black belts were conferred, three solidly built, tall men appeared in the halls of the Kodokan. It was obvious that they had come from another school of jujitsu. One of the guests introduced himself and his friends: "I am Daihachi Ichikawa, with me are Matsugoro Okuda and Morikiti Otake. We'd like to watch you work out. Is Mr. Kano here?"

"Our sensei is not here," Tsunejiro Tomita replied and, without further diplomacy, inquired, "Would our guests just like to watch and see what classes are like? Or did you come to incite conflict, as has already happened on more than one occasion?"

The behavior of the visitors convinced Kano's students that the guests had dishonorable intentions. Daihachi Ichikawa asked straight out whether Kano's students wanted to test their skill in a match. Remembering the Kodokan code, Tomita answered that a match was impossible without the permission of his sensei, to which Daihachi replied provocatively: "Avoiding a fight is apparently the chief feature of this school."

Then Shiro Saigo turned to his friend: "Let's take up these gentlemen's challenge and look upon this meeting as one among friends." Tomita shook his head and, with displeasure, said that their possible defeat could cause irreparable harm to their school and they would be compelled to abandon their sensei forever. Saigo, by contrast, thought that by declining the challenge they would demean the dignity of the school and, despite the risk, decided to fight, not wishing to suffer any further abuse. As Saigo was preparing for the match, two other students, Yokoyama and Yamashita, appeared at the door. Sensing the tenseness of those present, they realized that something dramatic was going on and, after examining the situation carefully, they also thought that they were better off not taking up the challenge without the permission of Dr. Kano, but it was too late. Saigo bowed to the heaviest and tallest of the visitors, Matsuguro Okuda. Okuda, extending his long, muscular arms, took the traditional hold and, pulling Saigo in to his body, tried to throw him and then tried to apply a choke hold or armlock, so as to dispel all doubt about his superiority. Kano's student, skillfully maneuvering and maintaining his balance, rendered all of Okuda's attempted offensives unsuccessful. Saigo seemed to be made of rubber. Unexpectedly counterattacking, he executed a throw, stunning his opponent. Falling the first time, the jujitsu master got up with lightning speed and attacked with redoubled energy, only to feel the hard tatami once again. This time he made no effort to get up and conceded defeat.

The news about the victory of Jigoro Kano's student over the jujitsu master spread rapidly throughout the city, and Shiro Saigo's name became famous far beyond Tokyo's city limits. It was he who served as the prototype for the famous literary and, later, cinematic hero Sanshiro Sugata, known to us through Akira Kurosawa's film *The Judo Genius* (known in the West as *Sanshiro Sugata*). Saigo was a phenomenally gifted fighter who could beat his own sensei, which in itself speaks of Kano's greatness as a teacher. The student surpassing the teacher—this is a sign of the quality of a coach's work that carries, it must be admitted, a hint of bitterness.

Modern Developments in Judo

Having gained the long-awaited—but most important—official recognition in his homeland, Jigoro Kano set out to realize his next grand plan—that judo be known around the world.

When one considers the magnitude of the task that Kano set before himself, it becomes apparent that he was a mover on a universal scale, a "man of the world." Getting ahead of ourselves, let us note that, in terms of recognition, fame, scale, and popularity, Kano achieved it all. Today there are around 200 member countries in the International Judo Federation, which was created in 1951. World championships and tournaments are held regularly. Judo has become an Olympic sport.

Women's judo occupies a firm position, and it was Kano who was at the forefront of this. He personally administered a test in fighting technique for his future wife, Sumako. They were married in 1891. The servants in their home, in addition to maintaining the household, also trained girls who wanted to practice judo. The experiment begun by the visionary Kano for attracting women to what was long a male activity was successful. The first competitions were held at the Kodokan. The women had their own "judo genius." The best woman over a three-year period, starting in 1925, was Hori Utako. Masako Noritomi, who entered the Kodokan in May 1925, would later become the author of a popular book, *Judo for Women,* which went through many editions. And Jigoro Kano's daughters did not besmirch the honor of their father's name: His eldest daughter, Vatanuko Noriko, later headed a judo section at the Kodokan, and Takasaki Atsuko also dedicated her life to her father's work. One of Kano's female students, Miyagawa Hisako, founded her own school, Sakuragako. All the women were extremely gifted. In 1926, a women's division was officially opened at the Kodokan. Kano always actively invited women to judo classes and would often say, "If you really want to understand judo, observe a woman training." However, for a long time, women's championships were not held in Japan itself, which in many ways had remained a conservative country.

The beginning of judo's westward movement was laid by Jigoro Kano himself on September 13, 1889, when he went to Europe to familiarize himself with the local physical education system and, at the same time, share his ideas on judo. By that time judo had become a fixed feature of Japanese culture for average Japanese and a required subject in school. There were active schools for military personnel, and Kodokan affiliates were opened. Jujitsu ceded its position to the new fighting system, but the confrontation continued. Only the stage where this debate was being played out changed. Europe was spoiled by English boxing and Greco-Roman wrestling, which had been transformed into a circus act, and, with savate in its arsenal of fighting styles and its familiarity with jujitsu thanks to traveling instructors who left Japan in search of income, Europe didn't care about yet one more "physical amusement." At first, Kano and his students met with a cold indifference from the public. But demonstrations, conducted in the presence of dozens of officials, stirred up tremendous interest, and many of those spectators would later become active in promoting judo.

During 1890, Jigoro Kano visited Lyons, Paris, Brussels, Vienna, Berlin, Copenhagen, Stockholm, Amsterdam, the Hague, Rotterdam, and London. Jigoro Kano's European trip bore fruit. A teacher and athlete exchange was begun, Kodokan affiliates were opened abroad, and judo schools opened up in European countries and, later on, in the United States. By the period after World War II, judo was practiced in 120 countries.

Judo started to grow most actively in France, where Kano first demonstrated his technique outside of Japan. The far-reaching consequences of this are felt to this day. In terms of sheer numbers and skill of its judoka, France occupies a leading position in Europe. Team France is one of the strongest in the world. History has preserved the name of Guy de Montgriliet, who opened a judo dojo in Paris in 1904. The first Frenchman to pass through the Kodokan was Le Prierre, who later headed a dojo in his homeland. A holder of the fifth dan, Keisiin Ishiguro moved to the French capital in 1924 and immediately opened up several dojos and held public demonstrations in neighboring countries. Professor Hanno Ri introduced the citizens of Germany and Switzerland to judo. In 1903 Jigoro Kano sent one of his best students to the U.S. There this student opened up a dojo that became so popular that Theodore Roosevelt himself took notice and attended classes. The Kodokan archives preserve the U.S. president's correspondence with Jigoro Kano.

The experienced Akitaro Ono, fourth dan, was teaching in Great Britain at the turn of the century. But while demonstrating judo he was forced to pass it off as jujitsu, so tightly did this relic from the samurai tradition retain its hold far from the homeland that had rejected it. For this reason, the authors of the first textbook on judo published in Europe, Irwin Hancock and Hatsukuma Osigashi, were forced to call their book *The Complete Guide to Jujitsu (Kano method)*.

In 1933, events occurred that stimulated the further growth of judo's popularity. Mr. M. Feldenkrais invited Professor Mikonosue Kawaishi to his newly opened club. Kawaishi was not only an expert in fighting techniques but also a subtle psychologist, who had sensed Europeans' longing for continuous rivalry, their aspiration for titles, signs of distinction, and other attributes that underscored the differences between people. He also felt it was necessary to differentiate students' levels of preparedness. Professor Kawaishi divided judo techniques into several different groups of varying difficulty and introduced a system by which a judoka who had passed his exams in the demonstration of technique earned the right to wear a belt of a certain color.

There is a common misconception that, of all the belts, the coveted black belt is the most prestigious one. In actuality, the highest mastery is denoted by the red belt, though Jigoro Kano himself, toward the end of his life, donned his white belt again in order to emphasize the depth and limitlessness of the secrets of the martial art he had created. To this day, in Europe, the following color scheme is used, and from this scheme you can tell a judoka's skill level. First are the six student degrees: sixth kyu—white belt, fifth kyu—yellow, fourth kyu—orange, third kyu—green, second kyu—blue, first kyu—brown. Then come the ten master degrees, or dans. Holders of the first five dans wear black belts that are distinguished by the number of white stripes at the end of the belt; dans six through eight wear red and white belts, and dans nine and ten wear red belts.

Time passed and along with successes arose the threat of problems connected with the management and organization of the training process for judoka, whose numbers were increasing on a daily basis, both in Japan and abroad. Starting in 1909, Jigoro Kano was forced to introduce entrance fees into the Kodokan and its affiliates and conduct paid exams for those wishing to improve their skill level.

The breadth of Kano's views on subjects related to physical education would not allow him to restrict himself to one sport, even his favorite. He created the Japan Amateur Athletic Union, which later became part of the International Amateur Athletic Federation. The appearance in 1911 of the Japan Amateur Sports Association was also due to Kano's efforts. As a passionate evangelist for various sports, he headed the Japanese National Olympic Committee in 1912 and became the first representative from Japan on the International Olympic Committee (IOC), which he remained a member of during the 1930s.

In 1922, Kano was able to fulfill a long-time dream—to organize the Kodokan Cultural Union, which was founded on the principles of judo. Ten years later, Jigoro Kano held the official title of minister of physical education. By that time, around 120,000 students were studying judo in schools, more than half of whom held black belts.

In 1938 a congress was held in Cairo on preparations for the Olympic games. It is to Kano's credit that the upcoming games were to be held in the Land of the Rising Sun, with judo as one of the sports. There are those who think that Kano himself objected to this, but it is difficult to agree with this idea, since, with his keen analytical mind, the professor must have realized how beneficial it would be to the development of judo if his brainchild were granted Olympic status.

Returning to his homeland on the *Hikawa Maru* ocean liner, the great master came down with a terrible case of pneumonia and died on May 4, 1938. Jigoro Kano gave judo lessons till his dying day, making daily visits to various Kodokan affiliates. Many people have testified to the fact that he was not only a great theoretician, but also a great practitioner.

After the death of Jigoro Kano, the job of popularizing judo among the better half of humanity was carried on by Risei Kano, Kano's son. Having become director of the Kodokan in 1946 (before that the institute was headed by Nango Jiro), he made a significant contribution toward strengthening judo's international standing. Japan's capitulation in World War II, and the subsequent occupation by American forces, defined the difficulty of the situation in which he was forced to function. The majority of athletic venues were destroyed in bombing raids, and starting in November 1945, American occupation forces headquarters put into effect a ban on practicing judo in official institutions, including schools. This ban was the product of the fear that the fighting system could have many unpleasant consequences for the authorities in case of civil unrest. In response, a measure was taken that led to the lifting of the ban. The Japanese coaches, in a show of loyalty to the authorities, taught the American regiments judo. They started to hold tournaments, but the turning point was 1948, when the Japan Judo Federation was formed and the first post-war national championships were held. In 1951, a physical education division for middle schools was formed within the federation, as well as the Pan Japanese Student Judo Federation.

The expansion of judo's geographical reach ultimately led to the world championship, which was held in 1956, in the homeland of this popular fighting system. The second world championship was held two years later, also in Japan. In this competition, the participants were not divided into weight categories. The strongest were Shokichi Natsui and Koji Sone. After a three-year hiatus, the third world championship was held in Paris in 1961, ending on a sensational note: The gold medal was won by a Dutchman, Anton Geesink, who beat Sone in the finals. This first failure by the creators of judo forced the Japanese to introduce weight categories. At the 1965 world championship there were four categories, and in subsequent championships there were five: under 63 kg, under 70 kg, under 80 kg, under 93 kg, and over 93 kg. Then the number of weight categories was increased to seven. For men the categories were under 60 kg, under 65 kg, under 71 kg, under 78 kg, under 86 kg, under 95 kg, and over 95 kg. For women, they became under 48 kg, under 52 kg, under 56 kg, under 61 kg, under 72 kg, and over 72 kg.

Presently competitions are held in the following weight categories: under 60 kg, under 66 kg, under 73 kg, under 81 kg, under 90 kg, under 100 kg, and over 100 kg for men, and under 48 kg, under 52 kg, under 57 kg, under 63 kg, under 70 kg, under 78 kg, and over 78 kg for women. There is also an open class, in which athletes of any weight may take part.

Judo debuted as an Olympic sport in 1964, when Japan was awarded the XVIII summer games. Judo attained final Olympic status at the 1972 Munich games.

Unfortunately, judo's creator did not live to see the time when judo would become a truly universal sport, popular around the world among children and adults, boys and girls, men and women. Millions of people of all ages practice judo. It would seem that his dream has come true. But Jigoro Kano saw his system least of all as a sport, although he no doubt understood that the longing of young people for competition would invoke the desire to compare one's strength with others and bring out the best in oneself. In his declining years, after attending a competition, Kano, very disappointed, gathered his students together and reproached them: "You fight like young bulls clashing horns. There was no refinement or elegance whatsoever in any of the techniques I saw today. I have never taught that kind of judo. If you are going to think only of winning through brute strength, that will be the end of Kodokan judo."

Today judo is mainly (in fact, virtually only) a sport. What we today call judo is far removed from what its originator had conceived and created. Jigoro Kano's theoretical developments and philosophical musings find no resonance in today's sport. We see only the tip of the iceberg, and only a tip that, under the influence of time, has changed its outline, acquiring new contours until it barely resembles the original form. Kano saw judo technique as a means to self-perfection on the path to achieving an ethical ideal. Today, alas, goals, points, and seconds have been given primary importance, causing the sport much harm. And even in judo's homeland, Japan, matters of prestige on the world tatami have pushed to the background the ideas that guided the great educator.

At the end of its most important competitions, the International Judo Federation produces videos with recordings of the opening and awards ceremonies and the most interesting moments of fighting. Photographs were taken at the 1989 world championship, when Toshihiko Koga, the winner of the under 71 kg division from Japan, ascended to the highest step on the winners' podium, earning a place in the history books. Along with demonstrating the highest level of technique on the road to the gold medal, Koga stunned everyone when, at the end of the final match, accompanied by a delicate girl who was serving as referee, the world champion cried, wiping the tears streaming down his cheek with the sleeve of his *judogi*. This was the reaction of a man who had devoted all his strength, both physical and moral, to judo fighting. Normal emotions that are natural and common for other sports don't seem entirely appropriate for judo, as Jigoro Kano conceived it.

As a follower of the samurai traditions, Doctor Kano, in his theoretical elaborations, used the ideas the eighteenth-century Zen patriarch Takuan set forth in two secret treatises communicated to the founders of the Kito Ryu school. Takuan claimed that victory could be achieved by combining firmness of spirit and concentration of will with a natural freedom of movement. An inner "void," a consciousness focused on nothing, an unwavering calm, and a high level of self-composure—these are the qualities that guarantee success to martial arts adherents. As we see, there is no room left for emotions.

Jigoro Kano saw the mottoes of the Kodokan Cultural Society, "The Most Efficient Use of Strength" and "Mutual Well-Being," as all-encompassing, with applications in economics, politics, and social relations. Jigoro Kano signed his philosophical works *Kiiti Sai* (Receptacle of the One). He believed the strengthening of the body and spirit of every human being through the practice of judo should lead to general prosperity. The principle of "mutual well-being" was elucidated by Kano as follows:

> If you approach the question from the point of view of the universal oneness and connectedness between things, then the goal—mutual well-being—must also be related to the means, that is, to the most efficient application of strength. Although here are two apparently different concepts, they essentially embody the same doctrine—the all-embracing unity to which the most successful application of force tends in all spheres of human activity—and nothing more.

In this way, Kano reveals himself as a follower of the classical Eastern philosophical and religious teachings, which are closely connected with the practice of martial arts. Nowadays this principle is merely proclaimed, existing as it were beyond the bounds of competitive activity that modern judo has come to represent.

What do we see today? Judo technique? Yes, without a doubt. But the spirit of judo as Jigoro Kano understood it is lacking now. Is this good or bad? There is no clear-cut answer to this question. That's how it has turned out. Such is the influence of time.

Judo as a sport has overshadowed the applied aspect of this primordial style of combat, yet judo does continue to be taught as a martial art and a self-defense method. The Kodokan program—which today is located on Kosug Street in the Bukinyo district in the largest dojo in the world (1,000 square meters), a seven-story building with five small and medium halls, where almost a hundred people can practice at a time—has its own research institute and includes several complexes for teaching fighting techniques and self-defense for both men and women.

Few people know that agents in the security organizations of Belgium, Germany, Holland, and France are required to study judo-hanim, a technique of traditional judo that a nonspecialist would have a very hard time distinguishing from jujitsu. This branch of judo exists independently and is very different from Kodokan judo, but even here, despite the fact that this system, which is full of striking actions and incorporates classical weaponry, is very effective in real-life situations, you can't help but notice the influence of the noble ideas of Jigoro Kano, jujitsu's reformer. Pain-causing pressure on the finger joints, eyes, mouth, and nose is forbidden, and choking techniques are permitted only with the help of clothing.

The original system of judo is cultivated by the Austrian Self-Defense Union. This system is one of paired kata that are carried out to the accompaniment of the rhythmic beats of a large drum, metronome, or tape recording of a drum and flute. The partners' movements, laid out in advance, transform the katas into a performing art spectacular. The applied effect of such activities, of course, is not great, but the prolonged—sometimes lasting three hours—reflex execution of movements delivers a powerful psychological discharge, combats stress, and removes tension and fatigue.

Judo unites people of various nationalities, tastes, and creeds. The multi-faceted nature of judo allows each person to find what only he or she needs. Much has been written about judo, but it is too early to write the final word—it's an inexhaustible topic. Judo, at over a hundred years old, continues to attract ever more admirers.

From the History of the Russian National Judo School

In 1961, the IOC approved the program of the XVIII Olympic games in Tokyo. Judo was included in the program. The Soviet Sambo Federation (sambo is a form of wrestling employing judo techniques) decided to train a team for the tournament in the Japanese capital. On October 18, 1962, the presidium of the Soviet Sambo Federation approved the team's lineup of judoka. It included V. Natalenko, O. Stepanov, T. Arabuli, A. Bogoliubov, R. Dzhagamadze, S. Stepanov (under 68 kg); A. Bondarenko, V. Pankratov, I. Tsipursky, A. Karashchuk, G. Nonikashvili, V. Kheisin (under 80 kg); and A. Kiknadze, A. Kibrotsashvili, D. Beruashvili, A. Lukashevich, B. Shaposhnikov, K. Romanovsky, P. Chikviladze, V. Usik, G. Shultz, and B. Mishchenko (over 80 kg). V. M. Andreev and V. F. Maslov were confirmed as the team's coaches.

The first gold medal to a European champion was won in 1962 in Essen, West Germany, by Anzor Kiknadze (open category).

The top step on the pedestal of honor in European championships was ascended by Aron Bogoliubov, Anatoly Bondarenko, Oleg Stepanov, Anzor Kibrotsashvili, Sergei Suslin, Vladimir Pokataev, Piruz Martkoplishvili, Roin Magaladze, Vladimir Saunin, David Rudman, Vitaly Kuznetsov, Sergei Melnichenko, Sergei Novikov, Givi Onashvili, Vladimir Nevzorov, Dzhibilo Nizharadze, Valery Dvoinikov, Temur Khubuluri, Avely Kazachenkov, Evgeny

Pogorelov, Aleksei Volosov, Aleksandr Yatskevich, Nikolai Solodukhin, Aleksei Tiurin, David Bodaveli, Grigory Verichev, Khazret Tletseri, Vitaly Pesnyak, Valery Divisenko, Khabil Biktashev, Tamaz Namgalauri, Yuri Sokolov, Igor Bereznitsky, Bashir Baraev, Koba Kurtanidze, Amiran Totikashvili, Sergei Kosorotov, Nazim Guseinov, Sergei Kosmynin, Tamerlan Tmenov, and Yuri Stepkin.

The Soviet judoka at the Olympiad in Tokyo were also a success. In judo's homeland, Aron Bogoliubov, Oleg Stepanov, Anzor Kinadze, and Parnaoz Chikviladze won bronze medals, taking the first step toward the Olympic heights.

Our Pride
Russian Men's Judo

Olympic Judo Champions

XX Olympic Games, August 26–September 11, 1972, Munich,
   West Germany
Shota Chochishvili (under 93 kg weight category)
Coach: G. M. Papitashvili
Head team coach: V. M. Andreev

XXI Olympic Games, July 17–August 1, 1976, Montreal, Canada
Vladimir Nevzorov (under 70 kg weight category)
Coach: Ya. I. Voloshchuk
Head team coach: V. M. Andreev

XXII Olympic Games, July 19–August 3, 1980, Moscow,
   Soviet Union
Nikolai Solodukhin (under 65 kg weight category)
Coach: M. G. Skrypov
Shota Khabareli (under 78 kg weight category)
Coach: O. M. Natelashvili
Head team coach: B. P. Mishchenko

XXV Olympic Games, July 27–August 2, 1992, Barcelona, Spain

Nazim Guseinov (Commonwealth of Independent States) (under 60 kg weight category)

Coach: A. Akhunadze

David Khakhaleishvili (CIS) (over 95 kg weight category)

Coach: A. B. Merabishvili

Head team coach: V. N. Kallin

World Champions

October 23–25, 1975, Vienna, Austria

Vladimir Nevzorov (under 70 kg weight category)

Coach: Ya. K. Koblev

Head team coach: V. M. Andreev

December 7–9, 1979, Paris, France

Nikolai Solodukhin (under 65 kg weight category)

Coach: M. G. Skrypov

Tengiz Khubuluri (under 95 kg weight category)

Coaches: G. M. Papitashvili, A. G. Kibrotsashvili

Head team coach: B. P. Mishchenko

September 3–6, 1981, Maastricht, The Netherlands

Tengiz Khubuluri (under 95 kg weight class)

Coaches: G. M. Papitashvili, A. G. Kibrotsashvili

Head team coach: G. I. Kaletkin

October 13–16, 1983, Moscow, Soviet Union

Khazret Tletseri (under 60 kg weight category)

Coach: V. I. Shkhalakhov

Nikolai Solodukhin (under 65 kg weight category)

Coach: M. G. Skrypov

Head team coach: G. I. Kaletkin

September 26–29, 1985, Seoul, South Korea

Yuri Sokolov (under 65 kg weight category)

Coach: Y. M. Kerod

Head team coach: G. I. Kaletkin

November 19–23, 1987, Essen, West Germany

Grigory Verichev (over 95 kg weight category)

Coach: Kh. M. Yusupov

Head team coach: G. I. Kaletkin

October 10–15, 1989, Belgrade, Yugoslavia

Amiran Totikashvili (under 60 kg weight category)

Coaches: Z. G. Kakharashvili, Sh. D. Khabareli

Koba Kurtanidze (under 95 kg weight category)

Coaches: A. G. Kibrotsashvili, B. S. Gogichashvili

Head team coach: V. N. Kaplin

July 25–28, 1991, Barcelona, Spain

Sergei Kosorotov (over 95 kg weight category)

Coaches: V. V. Arkhipov, Y. M. Kerod

Head team coach: V.N. Kaplin

September 28–October 1, 1995, Makuhari, Japan

Nikolai Ozhogin (Russia) (under 60 kg weight category)

Coaches: A.G. Gusev, S.A. Kabanov

Head team coach: V. N. Kaplin

Russian Women's Judo

The results for the women's team were more modest, but women's judo in Russia has been developing only since 1984. It is a pleasure to note that the very first victories at the international level belong to the women of the famous city on the Neva River.

The groundwork was laid by Elena Gushchina, who won a bronze medal in the open category at the 1989 European championship in Helsinki (coach: V. V. Antonov, head team coach: V. V. Kuznetsov). Elena Petrova won the second official medal—silver—in the under 61 kg weight category at the 1989 world championship in Ljubljana, Slovenia (coach: A. S. Korneev, head team coach: V. V. Kuznetsov). The third medal in the national team's collection, for second place, was won by Elena Besova in the under 72 kg weight category at the 1990 European championship in Frankfurt am Main, Germany (coach: A. S. Korneev, head team coach: V. V. Kuznetsov).

On Victory Day, May 9, 1992, in Paris, for the first time a Soviet woman judoka, Svetlana Gundarenko, who won in the over 72 kg weight category, ascended the highest step on the pedestal of honor at the European championships (coach: B. V. Shunkin, head team coach: E. A. Tiurin).

Finally, the only Olympic medal thus far (Barcelona, 1992), a bronze medal, belongs to Elena Petrova, who won in the under 61 kg weight category (coach: A. S. Korneev, head team coach: E. A. Tiurin).

The Best

At the close of the outgoing century, the Russian Olympic Committee made the suggestion to determine who the greatest coaches and athletes were that brought glory to Russia with their achievements. The best Russian judoka of the twentieth century was acknowledged to be Nikolai Solodukhin, decorated master of Soviet sports, Olympic champion, two-time world champion, European champion, five-time Soviet champion, and winner of the Spartakiad of the peoples of the Soviet Union.

The best coach in Russia of the twentieth century is Yakub Koblev, honored coach of the Soviet Union and doctor of pedagogical sciences, whose student won the highest award at the European and world championships and at the Olympic games.

The Competition Environment

Where Do the Matches Take Place?

Competitive duels (matches) in judo are conducted on tatami. In modern terms, the tatami is an area comprised of square mats made of polymer materials. In the beginning, judoka trained and competed on straw mats, whose hardness demanded great falling skill. The dimensions of the tatami are strictly defined. The minimum dimensions of the active zone are 8 by 8 m, and the maximum are 10 by 10 m. The active zone is assembled from green mats bound by red mats and is in turn surrounded by a layer of green mats. The width of this layer must be 3 m, to ensure safety; thus, the area of the mat around the active zone is called the safety zone.

Before the beginning of a match, the judoka must come out to the middle of the tatami and stand at a fixed spot. The participant called first puts on a blue jacket and walks up to the blue strip, and the second participant puts on a white jacket and walks up to the white strip. The strips (which can be colored adhesive tape) are around 10 cm wide by 50 cm long and are placed in the center of the active zone at a distance of 4 m from one another. The blue strip is to the right of the referee.

The Judo Uniform

The Japanese name of the judoka's uniform is *judogi*. It is made up of a kimono (jacket), *jubon* (pants), and *obi* (belt). The jacket, in contrast to the jacket worn in sambo, does not have sewn-on sleeves; furthermore, the jacket has no openings for the belt. The belt in judo is fastened over the jacket. The jacket, which must be made of cotton or a similar material, is rather loose, since throw techniques in judo are different from sambo fighting techniques. If you grab the jacket of a samboist and try to pull him or her in to your body, then, because the jacket is tight-fitting and made from a stiff, almost inelastic material, you pull in not only the jacket, but also the person wearing it.

Something completely different happens if we try the same action with a person wearing a judo jacket. Because of its loose fit, you first pull in the jacket and only then, when this "free move" has been completed, do you start to draw in the person in the jacket. This creates special demands in judo grabbing techniques.

Pursuant to Article 3 of the Competition Rules of the International Judo Federation, the judo jacket must be long enough to cover the hips and reach to the palms when hanging down alongside the body. The jacket must fold left over right and must be wide enough to fold no less than 20 cm below the lower part of the rib cage. The sleeves must be no longer than to the wrists and no shorter than 5 cm above the wrist. There must be a space of 10 to 15 cm along the entire length of the sleeve between the hand and the kimono.

The competition rules allow only two colors for a jacket, blue and white, so the audience and judges can tell the participants apart more easily. Previously, when the rules said a judoka could walk out onto the tatami in only a white kimono, the first opponent had to wear an extra red band, and the second opponent had wear a white one.

Today judo, like most sports, represents a market for athletic clothing and equipment, accessories, and advertising. Vendors, advertising firms, sponsors, and national federations vie for a particular team or athlete, creating a need for limits on company logos on jackets. The following labels and symbols are allowed on judogis: On the back is the Olympic abbreviation for the judoka's country (RUS, FRA, USA, etc.); on the left side of the chest, the country's symbol or flag (no larger than 100 sq cm) is shown. A manufacturer's logo (no bigger than 25 sq cm) may be placed below the jacket on the front of the left pant leg; a company label may also be on the shoulder (from the collar across the shoulder down the sleeves on both sides of the kimono, no larger than 25 cm in length and up to 5 cm wide). At the Olympics or world championship, a location marker (1, 2, 3, or 6 by 10cm) may be on the outer part of the left flap of the jacket. The athlete's last name may be written on the belt, on the outer side of the left part of the jacket, or on the front of the pant leg (no larger than 3 by 10 cm). The athlete's last name may be printed or sewn above the Olympic abbreviation (the inscription must be no greater than 7 cm high and 30 cm long).

Article 3 ("The Judo Uniform") of the rules is observed strictly at official competitions. Special judges are responsible for approving the athletes' clothing when they walk out onto the tatami. Besides the above-mentioned requirements, it should be noted that the pants must be long enough to cover the upper part of the ankle and no shorter than 5 cm above that. A belt in good condition—at least 4 to 5 cm wide and colored to correspond to the participant's rank—must be tied around the waist in a tight knot so as to firmly secure the jacket, preventing it from coming loose. The length of the belt must be such that, after wrapping around the waist twice and being tied in a knot, 20 to 30 cm of material is left over.

In addition, the female judoka must wear a long white or off-white T-shirt with short sleeves underneath the jacket. The T-shirt must be tucked in to the pants and be either white or off-white.

Etiquette

Judo begins with a bow, and judo ends with a bow. Respect for your opponent and for the judges is a requirement of any match. In judo the bow is given special attention as a tribute to the Japanese roots of this fighting style.

What Is the Correct Way to Bow?

There is a three-bow rule. The judoka makes the first bow before stepping out onto the tatami (upon entering the safety zone). Then, following the referee's signal, the second bow is made before crossing the red zone of the active area of the tatami. Finally, the third bow must be made while crossing the colored stripe in the center of the tatami. Before the match starts, before the command "Hajime!" ("Begin!") is given, the referee must make sure that the judoka are in the center of the tatami at the spots designated by the rules. The correct position is with the colored stripe behind the judoka.

When the match has ended and the outcome has been announced, the bowing ritual is carried out in reverse order. Bow, step back. Second bow upon leaving the red zone. Third bow upon exiting the tatami.

Special Preparatory Exercises

Special preparatory exercises incorporate elements of techniques or something similar to them. The basic objective of the exercises is to ensure that specific areas of the body are being worked. Depending on the targeted area, the exercises are divided into drilling, developmental, and combination categories.

1. Drill exercises are directed mainly at improving coordination through the mastery of various movements. This includes break-falling exercises, exercises with a partner and dummy, exercises in protecting and helping your partner while executing technical actions, acrobatic exercises, and imitation exercises.

2. Developmental exercises are directed primarily at developing and perfecting physical qualities specific to judo. These are divided into exercises to develop strength, speed, and endurance and their combinations; flexibility; aerobic exercise (lasting more than 5 to 8 minutes, at a heart rate of 130 to 150 beats per minute); aerobic-anaerobic exercise (2 to 5 minutes at a heart rate of 150 to 180 beats per minute); anaerobic lactate exercise (30 to 120 seconds with a maximum heart rate above 180 beats per minute); and anaerobic alactate exercise (up to 30 seconds at maximum intensity).

3. Combination exercises are meant to achieve two objectives at once: improving technical and tactical skills and raising the body's functional potential. Various technical-tactical moves are used as combination

exercises and are repeated many times in a specially selected regimen that ensures the development of the needed quality of techniques. Depending on the nature of the action, combination exercises are divided into exercises that increase the power of individual technical-tactical actions, groups of exercises, games of varying length and intensity, and matches that improve various techniques.

Drill Exercises

Break-Falling Exercises

Break-falling skills play a huge role both in judo classes and in the prevention of everyday injuries and injuries in actual fighting situations. It is especially important to master break-falling exercises at the beginning of judo study, since you can't progress to the study of such fundamental technical actions as throwing without a solid mastery of falling skills.

When teaching break-falling exercises, it is important to instill respect for partners/opponents in students during training.

Falling skills (without incurring injuries, broken bones, shock, or other harm) are acquired through repeated execution of exercises that are studied in a certain sequence and used in every workout.

Exercises with a Partner

The following are exercises for paired students:

- Push-ups. Your partner holds your legs. Your torso must remain straight, slightly bent at the waist. Your partner, while holding your legs, leans back slightly so as not to bend forward.
- Moving around on straight arms with partner holding legs.
- Moving around on bent arms with partner holding legs.
- Jumping around on arms in push-up position with partner holding legs.
- Crawling on all fours with partner on back.
- Reverse push-ups (chest up, hands behind you on floor).
- Moving around in reverse push-up position.
- Push-ups with partner sitting on your back.
- Push-ups with partner on his back, face up, holding arms straight up.

Motion is like regular push-ups, except you are pushing against partner's arms instead of floor.

- Push-outs: Lie on your back with arms outstretched; partner leans back against your hands. Flexing and extending your arms, use your partner's weight for resistance.

- One partner sits down with his back to the other, who is standing; first person lifts his arms up straight, pressing his palms into the palms of the other person. Either alternately or simultaneously, flex and extend your arms.

- Handstand push-ups with partner holding legs.

- Facing partner with arms held out in front, alternately flex and extend arms back and forth against one another.

- Partners stand a couple feet apart, facing each other and pressing against one another's outstretched hands. Without bending the arms, lean forward until you touch each other's chests. As you lean in, your arms will rise up toward the ceiling. Keep arms straight throughout.

Exercises for Developing Balance

The importance of balance in judo is difficult to overestimate. Therefore, much attention in preparing judoka must be devoted to exercises designed to develop and improve this important athletic quality.

The judoka should have well-developed coordination, including the ability to:

- Orient oneself in space
- Redirect one's movement
- Adapt to a changing situation and unusual tasks
- Anticipate the way in which a situation is going to change
- Maintain balance

Since maintaining the balance of a human body depends on the functioning of many of the body's internal systems, namely, vestibular (auditory), kinesthetic, visual, and tactile, the means for developing balance must allow for the optimal improvement of all systems that ensure the body's balance. A system consisting of general developmental gymnastics exercises with frequent changes in the structure and methodology for their application, games, and relays, other kinds of sports, special preparatory exercises, and fundamental technical actions ensures the development of the balance function.

General Developmental Gymnastics Exercises

This group includes gymnastics exercises with frequent changes in their structure and the way in which they are used. It is useful to apply them in lessons in such a way that, when you decide what the purpose of the general physical warm-up is, the exercises facilitate in many ways the development of the vestibular apparatus, thereby raising the balance level.

Below is a group of general developmental exercises to be performed both in motion and in place. These exercises are best done during warm-up. The duration of each exercise should depend on the students' level of readiness, from 15 to 20 seconds to 30 to 40 seconds. The exercises are done in combination with abrupt stopping and maintaining of balance, standing on one or two legs, and bringing the feet together, with eyes open and shut.

1. Walk around, vigorously, bending the head forward, backward, right, and left. Make two head motions for every step.
2. Walk around, moving the head in a circular motion, two motions per second.
3. Walk around. With each step, alternately look over your right and left shoulders, depending on which foot is forward (e.g., if the right foot is forward, you look over your right shoulder). Keep your gaze fixed on your partner, who is walking behind you.
4. Run while turning 360 degrees to the right and left.
5. Jump forward on two legs, making 360 degree turns.
6. Jump forward on one leg, making 360 degree turns.
7. Jump forward in a crouching position, making 360 degree turns.
8. Start out with legs apart, hands on your waist. Count one through four and alternate bending forward and backward on counts one and two and then right and left on counts three and four, two motions per second. After several repetitions, repeat the exercise with eyes closed.
9. Start out standing with legs apart, arms forward and to the sides. Count one to four. On one and two lift the right foot to the left hand. On three and four lift the left foot to the right hand.

10. Start out standing with legs apart, hands on your waist. Count one to eight. On one through four, circle the upper body clockwise, one motion per second; on five through eight, repeat the same number of motions counterclockwise.

11. Start out in a basic stance. Count one to four. On one, crouch down, bending the head forward. On two, lie down, head tilted back. Then on three, return to the crouching position, turn 360 degrees, and return to the basic stance on four.

12. Start out standing with legs apart, bending forward, hands in the air. Count one to eight. On one to four, circle your torso in a figure eight to the left, one motion per second. On five through eight, repeat to the right.

13. Start out with legs apart, hands behind your head. Count one to four. On one, turn your torso to the right, squatting on your left leg; on two, return to the starting position. On three turn your torso to the left, squatting on the right leg; and on four return to the starting position. One motion per second.

14. Start out with hands on your waist with your feet together. Count one to four. Bending forward, turn 360 degrees four times, one turn per second. After completing the exercise, maintain steady balance with your feet together. Repeat with eyes closed.

15. Start out with hands on your waist with your feet together. Count one to eight. Make four 360 degree turns with head bent forward on the first four counts; then make four 360 degree turns with head tilted back on the last four counts. After completing the exercise, maintain steady balance with your feet together. Repeat with eyes closed.

16. Start out in basic stance. In squatting position, hop in a circle until you return to the starting position. Repeat in the other direction.

17. Start out in basic stance. Jump in place, with your hands on your shoulders. Jump, turning 360 degrees clockwise, hands up. Jump in place, hands on shoulders. Jump turning 360 degrees counterclockwise, hands up. Then put your hands down.

18. Start out with legs apart. Lowering your hands, step with your right leg crossing over your left leg. Turn around in a circle. Repeat in the other direction.

19. Start out bending forward, hands on knees. With your eyes closed, turn 360 degrees, crossing one leg over the other. Do the exercise five times in each direction. After stopping, open your eyes, return to basic stance, and maintain balance 3 to 5 seconds.

20. Start out in basic stance. With your eyes closed, execute five 360-degree turning jumps then two forward somersaults. Turn in a circle and step backward, stepping into your starting position. Do the entire exercise with eyes closed.

21. Start out bending forward, hands on knees. Complete five 360 degree circles in small sideways steps and jump ten times on one leg, with your eyes closed in basic stance. Repeat on other side. Open your eyes. Maintain balance 3 to 5 seconds.

22. Start out with legs apart. Make five circular motions with the torso and five deep knee bends, then jump up into the basic stance. Maintain balance 3 to 5 seconds.

23. Start out in basic stance. With your right leg back and arms forward, balance on your left leg. Maintain balance 10 to 15 seconds. Repeat on other side.

24. Start out with your legs apart, standing on your toes with your arms forward. Count one to four, turning your head to the right and left. Maintain balance 8 to 10 seconds.

25. Start out standing on your toes, with your left leg and arms forward. Balance with your eyes closed, 10 to 15 seconds. Repeat on other side.

26. Start out balanced on one leg with eyes closed. Count one to four. On one and two lift your other leg to your chest, bending at the knee and grabbing your knee with your hands. On three and four lower the leg bent at the knee to starting position on one leg. Repeat on other side.

27. Start out balanced, standing on the toes with your heels raised high, one leg bent forward at right angle, and your hands out to the side. Balance in starting position 7 to 10 seconds. Repeat on other side. Repeat with eyes closed.

28. Start out standing with one foot behind the other, with the left heel touching the toes of the right foot (or vice versa), arms forward and apart. Balance in starting position and turn your head right and left, two motions per second. Repeat on other side. Repeat with eyes closed.

29. Start out in the same position as exercise twenty-eight. Balance in starting position while bending your head right and left, two motions per second. Repeat on other side. Repeat with eyes closed.

Games and Relays

Using games, relays, and play for developing balance helps improve nerve process control mechanisms, increasing the practitioner's strength and mobility and improving their accuracy and the variety of their functional activity. Furthermore, competition can be emotionally uplifting and can increase the students' vigor.

Here are some games students might try:

- Stand on one leg facing each other, hands behind your backs. The objective is to unbalance your partner by shoving with your shoulder, forcing him or her to put both feet down.

- The leader and all players move around, completing various somersaults, tumbles, and turns. The object is to tag one another.

- Count off, so that everyone is either a one or a two. Start out with the ones sitting on the shoulders of the twos. The pairs come together, with the people on top trying to bring down each other. After falling (or on command), the partners change places.

- Start with the players facing each other, hands on partners' shoulders (who has his arms on your shoulders). The object is to tag your partner's leg with your toes.

- Start out with all players forming a circle holding hands. An object of some sort (ball, chair, etc.) is placed in the middle. The circle starts moving either left or right, each person trying to force the people next to him to overturn the object. The player who overturns the object is out of the game.

- One partner get down on all fours. The other sits on the first partner's back, legs out to the sides. The person on the bottom tries to throw the one on top off his back.

- Again count off, so each student is a one or a two. The ones sit on the shoulders of the twos. The students on top pass a ball to each other. The ones below try to prevent them from doing so by moving in different directions. The players change places when the ball falls on the floor.

- Knee soccer (in squatting position).
- Split up into teams. The object is to throw a ball in the other team's goal. The ball can be touched with hands only. Holding the ball is forbidden.

Paired Exercises

Paired exercises are also useful for developing balance:

- One partner stands on the thighs of the other, who is sitting in a half-squatting position. The one on the bottom lies on his back, then rises up.
- Stand on the thighs of your partner, who is sitting with his back to the floor; sit on the shoulders of the person on the bottom, then stand up on their shoulders.
- Top person stands on the shoulders of partner, who is sitting or kneeling.
- One person lies with his hands up. His partner stands on his hands and balances by holding the bottom person's upraised legs.

Acrobatic Exercises

Acrobatic exercises are one of the most effective methods for coordination training and include the following exercises:

- Tumbling: Rolling (these resemble swinging on swings) then touching a support with various parts of the body, without tumbling over the head (for example, rolling on the back in a group)
- Somersaults: Circular motions like tumbling, but you turn head over heels forwards or backwards, bending forward and backward from various starting positions into various final positions
- Floor turns: Body moves forward, back, or to the side over the head (turning to the side is known as the "cartwheel")
- Flip turns: Jumping motions, turning the body back and forth over the head, pushing off with the hands and feet (turning from a dead start and a running start, round off, handsprings, etc.)

Tumbling exercises are performed at various parts of a class, depending on the task at hand. They are most often used for warm-up, since they help prepare the joints for difficult technical and tactical actions. In learning the difficult somersaults and rolls, you must use extra mats, any assistance needed, and protection.

Developmental Exercises

In applying exercises in this group, keep in mind that you can use exercises from various sports for developing and improving your physical qualities, but their ultimate effectiveness is determined mainly by the way they are applied.

Developing Strength

Despite the fact that judo is associated with the concept of the "victory of technique over brute strength," without sufficient strength, no judoka, no matter how refined in technique, can be assured of winning.

The most important abilities for judo are combination speed-strength skills or, more precisely, "explosive power," the ability to exert great strength in the shortest time.

In developing strength, the judoka mainly makes use of exercises with resistance. These include exercises with external resistance (barbells, dumbbells, machines, a partner) and weight-training exercises involving the judoka's own body (push-ups, pull-ups, rope climbing, horizontal bar, jumping, etc.)

Isometric (resistance) exercises facilitate the simultaneous tension of the greatest possible number of motion units of the active muscles. When you perform these exercises while holding your breath, they train the body to work under very difficult, oxygen-deficient conditions. These exercises are beneficial when working on ground-fighting techniques—holds and hold escapes.

Strength can be purposefully developed by tensing muscles to their maximum. There are several effective ways to create maximum tension.

The Maximum Effort Method

This method ensures an increase in maximum dynamic strength without a significant increase in muscle mass. This is very important for judoka, who must maintain a relatively constant weight within their weight category.

Each exercise should be done in several sets. For exercises that involve maximum and super-maximum resistance (when the weight is equal to 100 percent or more of the maximum for a given athlete) there should be no more than three repetitions in a set. Do two to three sets, with 3- to 4-minute rests between repetitions and 2- to 5-minute intervals between sets.

When doing exercises involving near-maximum resistance (90 to 95 percent of maximum weight), there may be five or six repetitions in one set, with two to five sets. Rest intervals between repetitions of exercises in each set should last 4 to 6 minutes, with 2- to 5-minute intervals between sets.

This method is applied during the training period of a yearly training cycle, and no more than two or three times a week. Weights above the maximum are used once every seven to fourteen days and are done in a decreasing regimen, using the assistance and protection of partners. This method is not recommended for people under the age of sixteen.

Repetitious Submaximum Effort Method

This method involves repetitions of less-than-maximum external resistance until the person starts feeling significant fatigue or can't go on.

In each set, the exercise is done without breaks. There may be anywhere from four to fifteen to twenty or more repetitions in each set. Between two and six series are done in a class. There are two to four sets in a series, with 2- to 8-minute breaks between sets and 3- to 5-minute breaks between series. The external resistance is usually 40 to 80 percent of the maximum for the given exercises. Movement is deliberate.

Keep in mind that when you use heavy weights and low repetitions you will be primarily developing maximum strength, or strength will grow along with muscle mass (which is not always desirable for judoka). Endurance grows with high repetitions and light weights.

Dynamic Effort Method

This method is used for developing speed-strength skills (explosive strength). The exercises should be carried out with relatively light weights (up to 30 percent of the maximum) with maximum speed.

To develop speed-strength there should be between fifteen and twenty-five repetitions per set. The exercise is performed in three to six series, with a break between series of 5 to 8 minutes.

Developing and Improving Endurance

In the process of any prolonged physical activity, sooner or later a person will begin to experience fatigue. The ability to fight off fatigue while maintaining a corresponding level of efficiency is the very definition of endurance—a physical quality that is essential for the judoka.

There are two different types of endurance—general and special. General endurance is necessary in any sport. It is the foundation upon which special endurance is built; special endurance reflects the specific nature of the athlete's sphere of competitive activity.

Training loads for developing general endurance are characterized by moderate intensity and significant volume. Up to 60 minutes of cross-country running or 30 to 40 minutes of randori are suitable. During rest periods, we recommend changing the type of activity and doing low-intensity exercises. For developing general endurance, sports where running is one of the main activities (football, basketball, handball) are also suitable. Organizing this process demands tremendous attention on the part of the coach, because judoka, due to the specific nature of their sport, play contact sports rather fiercely, leading to a higher incidence of injury.

At the training stage of the annual cycle, when the groundwork for general endurance is being laid, games can be included in the training program. When training right before a competition, games should be categorically excluded.

General endurance can be increased by specific means as well: moving games on the mat employing elements of fighting, various relays, team games like soccer (on your knees), or low-intensity fighting.

In judo, the basic needs of special endurance development and improvement are defined by the following temporal and physiological factors:

- The length of a competitive contest
- The maximum potential number of matches in the course of competitions
- A contest of strength at maximum intensity, alternately including virtually all muscle groups.

In this aspect, taking into account the rules of judo competition, the training process must be directed toward developing the ability to compete in five or six competitive matches (high-intensity, lasting 4 or 5 minutes, depending on age) in the course of a day.

In accordance with the differences in the nature of energy supply at different times when the muscles are active, it is customary to divide training into aerobic (involving external breathing) and anaerobic (using chemical reactions without oxygen) components of endurance. The anaerobic mechanisms are most significant at the beginning stages of activity (from several seconds up to 2 minutes), as well as in short-lived exertions of high intensity. The intensification of anaerobic processes also occurs when any change occurs in the intensity with which an exercise is being performed, when blood circulation in the active muscles has been cut off (tightening, holding one's breath, static tension). Aerobic mechanisms play an important role in prolonged activity (reaching peak levels by three to five minutes), as well as during warm-down.

The primary factor of special endurance is anaerobic production, which ensures muscle activity at the very beginning, in the first few seconds. Without getting into the details of the biochemical and physiological mechanisms of this difficult and not thoroughly understood process, we will look at training methods designed to address these issues.

Improving the Alactate Special Endurance Mechanism

This includes throwing a dummy or partner and training matches. The training matches may last 15 seconds at a maximum tempo then 1 to 2 minutes at a slow tempo, in a series of six. The same regimen can be used for throwing either a dummy or a partner. During periods of activity, the heart rate must exceed 180 beats per minute; the rest of the time it should be at 150 to 160 beats per minute. This will ensure the required training effect.

After these types of classes, you should increase your intake of rich creatine phosphates (meat and dairy products), and take methionine and vitamin B_{15}.

Improving the Lactate Special Endurance Mechanism

This demands significant exertions of the will. Training matches (or series of special exercises) are the basic method for improving this mechanism. The following two regimens are recommended.

The main purpose of the first regimen is to increase glycolysis capacity. The exercises last 1 to 2 minutes; each series has three repetitions. Exercises should be performed at near-maximum intensity, with a rest interval of 2 minutes after the first rep and 1 minute after the second one. A judoka should have rest intervals of 15 to 20 minutes between series, depending on the judoka's weight category. The time should increase with higher weight categories. In addition, in the last reps of the series, you can use difficulty in breathing (special masks) right up to holding one's breath.

The main purpose of the second regimen is to increase glycolysis strength. In this regimen, one repetition lasts 30 to 50 seconds; there are three repetitions in a series, with breaks between repetitions of 1 to 2 minutes. There should be no more than four series. Breaks between series should be 15 to 20 minutes, depending on the judoka's weight class. The time should increase with higher weight categories.

In both cases the heart rate reaches the maximum; during breaks calm walking and breathing exercises should be done.

Improving the Aerobic Special Endurance Component

Training matches can be used for this as well, but at a 70 to 80 percent intensity level (heart rate should be around 170 to 180 beats per minute). The exercise lasts $1^{1}/2$ minutes. There are eight or nine reps (five to eight for heavyweights). Breaks are determined according to the heart rate (as a rule, one to two minutes). By the beginning of the next repetition, the heart rate should be no lower than 130 to 140 beats per minute. When doing two series in a training session, the break between them should be 15 to 20 minutes.

Speed Skills

The most common way to improve reaction speed is the repetition method, which calls for repeated performance of exercises when signaled. This method facilitates improvement of sensory and motor reactions. Subsequently, with this method, reaction speed stabilizes and further improvement occurs with efficiently.

As a counterbalance to this method, you can use the games method, which involves executing tasks under conditions of constant and random situation changes and the counteraction and response of partners. For this, relays and outdoor and athletic games, including quick reaction to sudden signals, can be used as exercises.

The general principle for selecting exercises is the variety of conditions, their gradually increasing level of difficulty, and their approximation to the specific nature of the judoka's main activity.

The sensory method is a method based on the close connection between reaction speed and the ability to distinguish very small time intervals (tenths and hundredths of a second). People who can detect microintervals of time are generally known for their fast reaction time.

Complex reactions are divided into reactions to a moving object and reactions of choice. These types of reactions are typical in judo. Most of the time spent in reacting to a moving object (more than 80 percent) goes to visual perception. This ability is learned through training. For this, exercises that involve reaction to a moving object are employed. In performing these exercises, it is necessary to gradually increase the speed at which the object moves and decrease the size of the object.

Reaction of choice involves choosing the required moving object from a set of possible objects in accordance with a change in the behavior of a partner, opponent, or situation. This is a much more difficult kind of reaction. Here reaction time depends in large part on the athlete's reserve of tactical actions and techniques and on the ability to instantly choose the best objects.

In order to improve the time for reaction with a choice, it is necessary to gradually complicate the nature of the responses and the conditions in which they are carried out and develop an ability to anticipate your opponent's actions and forestall their initiation; that is, to react not so much to your opponent or partner as to her barely perceptible preparatory movements and outward appearance (stance, gestures, emotional state). An important task in working with speed skills is to anticipate the formation of a speed barrier, and, if one emerges, to destroy or weaken it.

In this case, when working with skilled athletes we recommend decreasing the load capacity in competitive exercises and increasing the proportion of speed-strength and other general training and special training exercises.

Combination Exercises

Exercises in this group involve mainly increasing the power with which technical-tactical actions are executed and improving the body's energy supply mechanism, which is utilized during practice, training, and competitive matches.

Practice matches help judoka to master, strengthen, and perfect technical and tactical skills and abilities and cultivate essential physical and volitional qualities, and to acquire and maintain a high level of preparedness.

The Drill Match

Directed at the mastery of new material, drill matches are carried out according to the given task. Your partner does not offer full resistance and occasionally creates conditions for the trainee that are favorable (in accordance with the task) for performing a technique. The drill match is geared toward mastering a single technique or the combination of two or three techniques. The match is conducted at a slow or moderate pace so that you may have better control over your actions. The duration of the exercise depends on the task of the workout. Fatigue should not settle in while performing this exercise, since this will hinder correct mastery of the technique.

If the exercise is not executed precisely, the match is interrupted to correct mistakes. In the drill match, your partner should help you in completing the task.

These matches should be carried out at the beginning of the main part of class. They are used mainly during the warm-up period and at the preliminary training stage in the main period.

The Drill-Training Match

These are basically for improvement of particular techniques under much easier conditions than those of an actual match. They are carried out with various objectives directed at further mastery and strengthening technical and tactical actions, eliminating weak areas, developing physical qualities, and refining certain fighting skills with specific opponents.

In the drill-training match, the student polishes his all-around skills, counterskills, and defense. The judoka should strive to get in various situations and find the right way out of them. As in the drill match, the drill-training match may be interrupted to point out mistakes, if necessary, but this should not be abused.

The time allotted for drill-training matches depends on the nature of the lesson. If it is a practice training class, then the match is conducted at the beginning of the main part; if it is a training lesson, it is conducted at the end, after the students have finished their training matches and rested.

Drill-training matches are most often used in the training period, in the preliminary and immediate training stages in the main period of a training year.

Training Match

In these matches, technique, tactics, and physical and volitional skills are developed under conditions that approximate those of competition. All actions are carried out with a keen eye toward their correct execution. The training match should not be interrupted for commentary. In extreme cases, it is OK to do so in the course of fighting. Comments should be clear and concise.

Applying the Competitive Games Method in Judo Training

The competitive games method in physical education is a way of acquiring and expanding one's knowledge, abilities, and skills, and the development of motion and moral-volitional qualities under conditions of a game or competition. Its application allows you to address a wide range of tasks under the most varied conditions. The following are characteristics of this method:

- The existence of rivalry and emotionality in motor activities
- Unpredictability, both in the conditions and actions of the participants
- A show of maximum physical exertion and mental focus
- Striving to win under fixed rules
- The use of various motor skills applicable under the specific conditions of a game or competition

This method facilitates the accumulation of motor experience that makes mastering the program material easier. There is a considerable emotional charge inherent in competitive games tasks, which serves as an effective means not only for physical development but also inner growth. The object of the tasks is to develop both physical qualities and specific abilities and skills in the students.

Tasks for Development of Athletic Performance

Objective: to strengthen maneuverability skills, develop a feeling of distance in a competitive situation.

Participants form a circle, taking one another's arms, joining them at the elbows or the wrist joints. Half of the participants stand facing the inside of the circle, the others face outside. Upon the coach's command, everyone begins moving together, first right, then left; when they hear a clap, each person starts moving in his own direction, that is, toward the inside or the outside of the circle. The person who can't hold his own and crosses the line of the circle by even one step is out of the game.

The game continues as long as the size of the circle allows the players to grab each other's arms. The team with the most people left at the end wins.

Objective: to develop the ability to execute a grab correctly under game-like conditions, to develop arm strength.

The players form pairs standing opposite one another and prepare to grab a certain part of their rival's body. Each player in a pair must be the first to grab with both hands the body part that was agreed upon in advance: wrists, torso, back, neck, legs, etc.

Order of the competition: (1) Some participants are attackers, others defenders; (2) roles are switched; (3) everyone is an attacker. The position of the hands is arbitrary.

Victory occurs only when the defined body part is grabbed. The winner is the one who completes the task first and correctly. The team with the most members to execute the grabs wins.

1. Objective: to develop stability and improve coordination and endurance.

The teams form a single file line or circles. When the signal is given, the players begin the following exercises:

- Forward somersaults, legs crossed; repeat after turning 180 degrees
- Move from basic stance to lying down position using your hands
- Ten clapping push-ups

The team that completes the exercise first wins. The contest has two variations: Whoever completes a fixed number of exercises first wins, or whoever completes the most exercises in a fixed amount of time.

2. Objective: to develop very simple fighting skills under standard conditions with a limited number of permissible actions.

The participants lie down opposite each other in pairs, placing the elbows of their right or left arms on the floor and joining hands. Players must fight with one hand, holding the other hand behind the back. The elbow must remain on the floor.

The fighting starts when the coach gives the signal. Each player tries to beat his or her opponent by bending the opponent's hand toward the mat. The team whose players score the most victories wins.

3. Objective: to strengthen fighting skills in a competitive situation.

Team participants form a single file line and place their hands on each other's shoulders, with one foot behind the other for support. The fighting begins when the coach gives the signal. While leaning on his or her rival's shoulders, each participant tries to force him or her over the line or a defined area (mat, circle, etc.). Whoever is able to knock his or her rival off the line wins. The winning team is the one with the most victories.

4. Objective: to improve strength, dexterity.

The players on one team grab each other's arms and form a circle. Their rivals are inside the circle. When the signal is given, the players in the circle try to break through the circle in pairs. Then the teams switch roles. No more than one pair may pass through a breach in the circle. The team with the most players to break through the circle wins.

5. Objective: to develop strength, dexterity, and reaction speed.

Both teams form a circle. One player stands in the middle with his arms at his sides. The others sit close to the player in a circle, legs crossed, and reach out their arms toward him. The player falls toward the outstretched arms of the players sitting down, who have to push him away. The player who is unable to push him away changes places with him.

6. Objective: to develop basic physical qualities in a competitive situation.

The players stand in pairs on one leg, holding their other bent leg by the toes, facing each other in a circle 6 to 12 ft in diameter. Each player hops on one leg and shoves the other player with his shoulder, trying to force his partner to lose his balance and put his other foot down. Players can hop only within the circle. Players must shove each other only with their shoulders. The player who forces his partner out of the circle or forces him to put his other foot down, wins. The winners form new pairs until a certain amount of time has passed.

7. Objective: to develop fighting skills, dexterity, strength, and coordination. Members on a team lie down next to each other, with their heads in different directions, linking half-bent arms. When the signal is given, the players raise their legs, link them together, and try to force each other to roll over backwards.

8. Objective: to develop dexterity, coordination, speed, and endurance. Participants divide up into two teams, "predators" and "prey." The predators hold hands, forming a chain, and pursue the other players, trying to tag them while they scatter. Only the players at either end of the chain can tag the others. The players who get tagged are out of the game.

The players being chased can break through the chain or slide under the other players' hands. If the chain is broken, a player cannot be tagged.

9. Objective: to develop speed, dexterity, and coordination. All players form a column. Each player grabs the belt of the person in front of him or her. The first player is the "head"; the last person is the "tail." When the coach gives the signal, the head tries to chase the tail. After a certain amount of time, the teams change places.

Important Training Tips

In order to design the training process in a rational way, patterns of human development and scientifically based approaches should be taken into account when formulating training aims. The information below will help to plan the training regimen, increase its effectiveness, and help avoid ineffective work.

Muscle strength follows a twenty-four-hour cycle. Muscles are strongest between 3:00 PM and 4:00 PM. In January and February, muscles increase in strength at a slower rate than in September and October. The best conditions for muscle activity are at a temperature of 68° F. Outside temperature influences speed capabilities. Maximum speed occurs at 68 to 72° F. At 60° F, speed decreases by 6 to 9 percent.

After about fifteen to twenty years old, range of motion (flexibility) decreases; improving this quality is much more difficult after this age. The body is at its least flexible in the morning after you wake up; thereafter flexibility gradually increases, reaching its maximum during the day (between

12:00 PM and 7:00 PM), but by evening flexibility is again lower. Warm-up exercises, massage, and heat treatments (warm bath, hot shower, or heat massage) can help to significantly increase range of motion. A decrease in the movement of joints occurs when the muscles are cold and after eating.

When stretching exercises cease, flexibility gradually decreases, and in two to three months returns to its original level. Therefore, you should not take more than one to two weeks off from training.

Where Does the Study of Judo Technique Begin?

Despite judo's one hundred-plus-year history and the tremendous experience built up over that time by experts from various countries, where to begin the study of judo technique remains an open question. Various approaches to beginning study produce positive results.

At the Kodokan, a classification of standing fighting techniques has been adopted that is comprised of five blocks of eight techniques each (Gokyu-No-Waza). The judoka, in mastering the throws included in each block and then demonstrating his level of mastery in a test, earns the right to receive the next student degree (kyu). The color of a judoka's belt indicates his level of technical preparedness: fifth kyu, yellow belt; fourth kyu, orange belt; third kyu, green belt; second kyu, blue belt; first kyu, brown belt.

Table 1. Classification of Standing Fighting Techniques

FIFTH

Kyu No.	Technique
1	Foot Sweep
2	Knee Wheel
3	Sweeping Drawing Ankle
4	Minor Hip Throw
5	Major Outer Reaping
6	Minor Underarm Hip Throw
7	Major Inner Reaping
8	Minor Shoulder Throw

FOURTH

Kyu No.	Technique
9	Ko-Soto-Barai
10	Minor Inner Reaping
11	Hip Wheel Throw
12	Collar-Grab Hip Throw
13	Sliding Foot Sweep
14	Body Drop
15	Sweeping Hip Throw
16	Inner Thigh Reaping Throw

THIRD

Kyu No.	Technique
17	Outer Hook
18	Torso-Grab Hip Throw
19	Side Drop
20	Major Side Wheel
21	Corner Reversal
22	Sweeping Drawing Ankle to Rear Leg
23	Circle Throw
24	Shoulder Wheel Throw ("The Mill")

SECOND

Kyu No.	Technique
25	Corner Reversal
26	Valley Drop
27	Similar to Maki-Komi
28	Scoop Throw
29	Wheel Throw (Throw Opponent on Hip)
30	Major Wheel
31	Maki-Komi
32	Floating Drop

FIRST

Kyu No.	Technique
33	Floating Throw
34	Backwards Throw
35	Side Falling Separation
36	Back Falling Throw
37	Counter Throw to Hip Throw
38	Twisting Back Throw
39	Corner Drop
40	Side Hook

Chart 1 shows how the techniques are distributed in standing position. This is the result of many years of Kodokan practice.

Chart 1. Kodokan

No.	Technique	Throws	Percentage
1	Ashi-Waza	12	29
2	Koshi-Waza	11	28
3	Te-Waza	4	10
4	Kata-Waza	2	5
5	Sutemi-Waza	11	28
	Total:	**40**	**100**

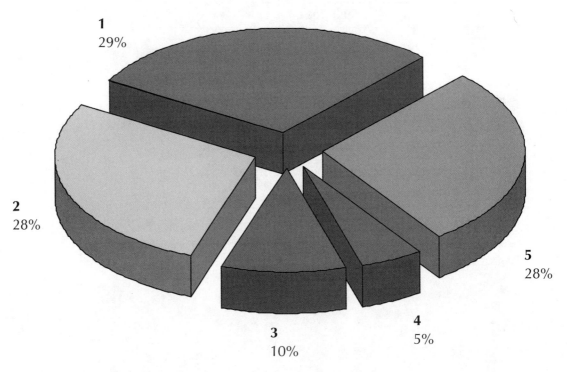

In Holland, they use the classification system created by Professor Miko-nosuke Kawaishi. According to this classification, there are sixty standing fighting techniques (nage-waza) subdivided into:

- Fifteen leg-fighting techniques (ashi-waza)
- Fifteen hip-throw techniques (koshi-waza)
- Nine hand-fighting techniques (te-waza)
- Six shoulder throws (kata-waza)
- Fifteen falling throws (sutemi-waza)

There are seventy-one ground-fighting techniques (permitted in competition), subdivided into:

- Seventeen holds
- Twenty-nine choking techniques
- Twenty-five armlocks

Chart 2 shows the percentage distribution of techniques recommended for study by Professor Kawaishi.

Chart 2. Kawaishi

No.	Technique	Throws	Percentage
1	Ashi-Waza	15	25
2	Koshi-Waza	15	25
3	Te-Waza	9	15
4	Kata-Waza	6	10
5	Sutemi-Waza	11	25
	Total:	**56**	**100**

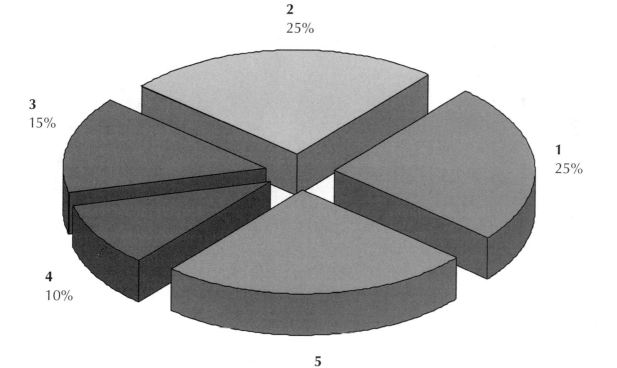

Other classifications have also proven the effectiveness of studying techniques in a particular order (Mifune classification, Tadai Koike classification, Anton Geesink classification, and others).

In our view, the modern approach to resolving the problem of content and order of study must take into account competitive practice. Chart 3 gives an idea regarding the approximate distribution of standing fighting techniques in modern competitive practice.

Chart 3. Competitive Practice

No.	Technique	Percentage
1	Ashi-Waza	35
2	Koshi-Waza	13
3	Te-Waza	19
4	Kata-Waza	23
5	Sutemi-Waza	10
	Total:	**100**

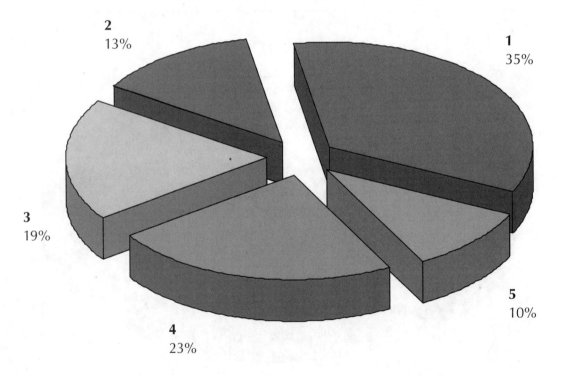

An analysis of the charts shows an undeserved lack of attention to the group of shoulder throws (kata-waza) at the beginning stage of mastering the judo technical arsenal, despite the frequency of their use in actual competition.

Professor E. M. Chumakov has worked out a classification of sambo fighting techniques that divides standing fighting into three subclasses: arm throws, leg throws, and torso throws (see diagram below). In turn, arm throws are subdivided into three groups: breaking balance, one-leg-grab throws, and two-leg throws. Leg throws are subdivided into five groups: drops, sweeps, throws, reapings, and back throws. Torso throws are subdivided into two groups: shoulder and chest throws.

Standing Fighting Techniques

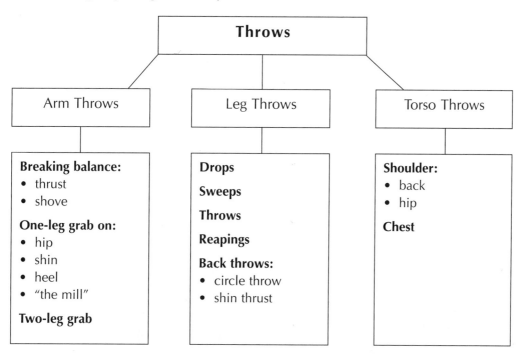

The use of this classification system in judo is, in our view, entirely correct, since the roots that gave life to sambo are tightly interwoven with those of judo and the arsenal of standing techniques is practically identical.

An analysis of the technical arsenal of high-level judoka suggests the a priority in the use of judo techniques as shown in the following charts (see charts 4, 5, and 6). In competitive practice, judoka most often use the following technical arsenal in order to achieve victory. In ground fighting, however, holds produce the best results. The percentage of clean victories from armlocks and choking techniques is significantly lower and approximately identical. In standing fighting, the most prized techniques are the drop (usually the major outer drop), shoulder throws from a standing position and kneeling, inner reapings, inner thigh reapings, and leg-hold throws. Sweeps are used mainly as a set-up attack move in a combination.

Chart 4. Frequency of Standing Judo Attack Actions

No.	Technique
1.	Shoulder throws
2.	Inner thigh reapings
3.	Kneeling shoulder throws
4.	Minor inner hooks or reapings
5.	Body drops
6.	Major outer drops, major outer reapings
7.	One-arm shoulder throw
8.	Reversals and circle throws
9.	Advancing foot sweeps
10.	Two-hand reapings
11.	Twenty other techniques

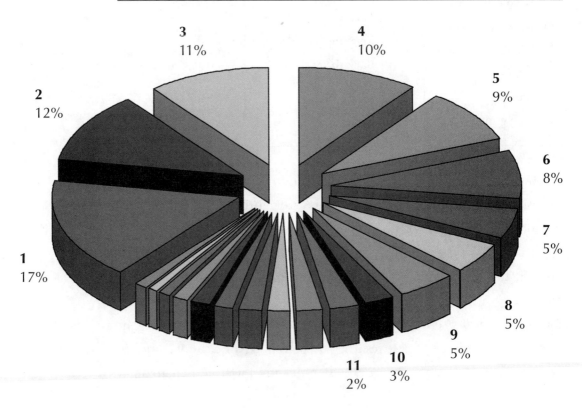

Chart 5. Frequency of Application of Judo Technique Sets

No.	Technique
1.	Shoulder throws
2.	Sweeps
3.	Hooks or reapings
4.	Body drops
5.	Reapings
6.	One- or two-hand leg throws
7.	Throws involving preliminary fall by attacker

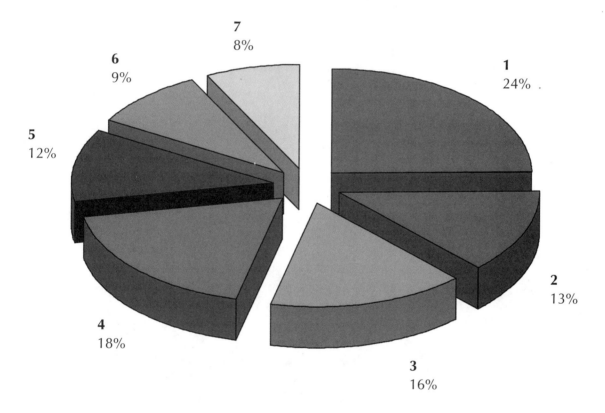

7
8%

6
9%

5
12%

1
24%

2
13%

4
18%

3
16%

Chart 6. Effective Standing Competitive
Judo Technique Arsenal

No.	Technique
1.	Shoulder throws
2.	Inner thigh reapings
3.	Kneeling shoulder throws
4.	Major inner reapings or hooks
5.	Body drops
6.	Major outer drops, major outer reapings
7.	One-arm shoulder throws
8.	Reversals and circle throws
9.	Advancing foot sweeps
10.	Minor inner hooks
11.	Hip throws
12.	Twenty other techniques

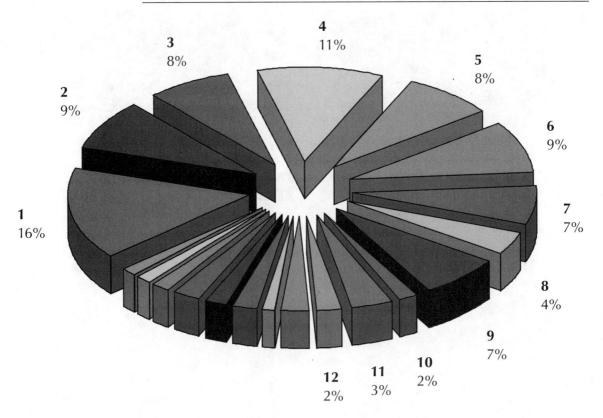

When talking about a judoka's technical skill, you must think of his training in terms of mastering the entire arsenal of techniques. However, even the most qualified and titled judoka have a limited number of techniques in their competitive arsenal (two, three, or—less frequently—four standing techniques and one to three ground-fighting techniques). Nonetheless, a significant number of various setups allow them to achieve tremendous results with their crowning techniques.

Therefore, at the beginning stage of study, the judoka must master the entire arsenal of basic techniques at his or her skill level. In the process of further development, it is necessary to limit one's fighting arsenal to those technical actions that will be determined in the process, taking into consideration the judoka's individual traits, fighting style, and competitive practice.

Basic Concepts

Terminology

It is impossible to verbally communicate all the technical subtleties of judo. Only through constant repetition of techniques under the guidance of an expert coach and through competitive experience can the judoka get a proper sense of the various facets of technique. Even an action as familiar to everyone as putting on a vest or jacket, which everyone has known how to do since childhood and which presents no difficulties, is extremely difficult to fit into the framework of instruction. In order to make understanding judo technique easier, we will use the following definitions.

Attacker (tori): The person executing the technique.

Defender (uke): Partner, opponent.

Far: With respect to tori's right hand or foot, *far* means that tori has his left side turned toward uke (is on uke's right side). With respect to tori's left arm or leg, *far* means that tori has his right side turned toward uke (is on uke's left side).

Same: With respect to the sleeve, lapel, etc., means that the right arm grabs the opponent's judogi from the right side, or the right hand grabs the opponent's right leg. Accordingly, the left hand grabs the opponent's judogi from the left side, or the left hand grabs the opponent's left leg.

Near: With respect to tori's right arm or leg means that tori has his right side turned toward uke (is on uke's left side). The term *near* with respect to tori's left arm or leg means that tori has his left side turned toward uke (is on uke's right side).

The directions *forward, backward,* and "to the side" are used in relation to uke. The directions for executing an action "away from one's body," "toward one's body," "to the right," "to the left," and "behind oneself" are used in relation to tori.

Rules of Conduct on the Mat

Despite the fact that judo is a contact fighting sport in which armlocks, choke techniques, and big and powerful sweeping throws are allowed and training and competition matches require a complete mobilization of forces from the judoka, judo is far from the leading injury-causing sport. Nevertheless, observing safety measures during classes is the basis for success in understanding the secrets of judo. Students must remember several simple rules of conduct during training:

- Do not sit with your back to the center of the mat.
- While working on throws, you must be situated so that your partner's fall flows from the center of the mat to the edges.
- When falling, do not stick out a straight arm to cushion the fall.

Combining Techniques

Victory in a competitive match can be achieved in various ways. The simplest—yet least reliable—way is a single-technique attack (A). The uke's skilled defensive actions, however, as well as his ability to anticipate the beginning and substance of an attack, often neutralize tori's efforts in a single-technique attack.

The same technique may also be used in other ways. For example, in combination with preparatory techniques (a1, a2, a3 . . . an), when an opponent's defensive reaction creates a favorable dynamic situation for executing technique A (e.g., the combination a1A, a2A, . . . anA). Or in combinations where the beginning of technique A makes it easy to execute other techniques, or as a result of uke's defensive actions (combinations like Aa1, Aa2, . . . Aan).

The illustrations show the basic technical and tactical sets of technique combinations in judo:

1. Those that include a few preparatory techniques that lay the groundwork for the basic (closing) combination technique.

2. Those that create opportunities, with an attempted preparatory technique, to continue the attack with several techniques, each of which could be used as a final throw.

The study and mastery of these combinations should help judoka to master their skills and shape the combination fighting style that is preferred in modern judo.

Break-Falling Techniques (Ukemi)

Despite the fact that the mats have an even surface and are rather thick, the ability to fall in a way that prevents injury requires special skills in judo. It has been said that judo begins with a bow. It would be more correct to say that judo begins with a fall. Learning technique in judo begins by studying break-falling techniques.

Sideways Break-Falling

Let's take a situation where the fall is on the right side. The judoka will have to assume the following final position: lying on the side, right arm straight, palm down away from torso at an angle of approximately 45 degrees. The other arm is away from the body and raised upward. The head does not touch the mat; the chin is tucked in to the chest, legs are bent, knees spread apart. Before assuming the final position, even before the torso touches the mat, the judoka must strike the mat forcefully with his hand. It is important to have the fingers close together and straight and the arm fully extended. This pre-emptive strike against the mat has a shock-absorbing effect that prevents internal organs from getting knocked around during the fall. Having the chin tucked in to the chest keeps the head from hitting the mat and helps prevent a concussion. Spreading the legs out protects the knee joints and groin from getting hit.

There is one other way of avoiding injury to the lower extremities. After the preemptive strike with the straightened arm against the mat and landing on your side, raise your straightened legs up in the air.

Note that the final positions given here are the ideal. During workouts, and even more so during competitions, it won't always be possible to follow all recommendations. The most important criterion for correctness of execution of break-falling techniques is if no injury is incurred from the fall! Here is the order of study for this technique:

1. Study and memorize the final position.
2. Work on the shock-absorbing strike.
3. Fall on your side from a sitting position.
4. Fall on your side from a crouching position.
5. Fall on your side over a partner who is on all fours.
6. Fall on your side from a standing position.
7. Fall on your side from a standing position while jumping.
8. Fall on your side in a somersault, holding your partner's hand.
9. Fall on your side from your partner's throw.

Backward Break-Falling

In order to ensure safety while falling backwards, the judoka must take up the following position: chin tucked in (this prevents the back of the head from striking the mat, which may result in a concussion), knees together and pulled up to the stomach (this protects the hip areas of the spinal column and kidney from hitting the mat), arms straight and away from the body at about a 45 to 60 degree angle (palms facing the mat, fingers together). Before taking up this backward falling position, even before the back touches the mat, the judoka must land a preemptive strike against the mat with her arms so as to absorb the shock from the fall and protect the internal organs from harm. Here is the order of study for this technique:

1. Study and memorize the final position.
2. Work on the shock-absorbing strike.
3. Fall on your back from a seated position.
4. Fall on your back from a crouching position.
5. Fall on your back over your partner, who is on all fours.

6. Fall on your back from a standing position.

7. Fall on your back from a standing position while jumping.

8. Fall on your back in a somersault.

9. Fall on your back from your partner's throw.

Forward Break-Falling

There are two basic methods in forward break-falling. The first one is in principle no different than techniques used in sideways or backward falling. The most important thing here is also the shock-absorbing strike on the mat. For this, the bent arms are turned palms facing forward (fingers pressed firmly together) and are the first part of the body to touch the mat. The straightened legs are slightly spread apart.

The second method resembles how volleyball players land after hitting the ball in a fall. Arms are slightly bent, palms facing out, fingers spread apart. The head tilts back and turns to the side. The legs go back by bending at the waist. The fingers are the first body part to touch the mat; then the person falls smoothly to his chest, then stomach, and finally the hips touch the mat. This method protects the internal organs from shock and the face and knee joints from injury.

Why Does My Opponent Fall?

A person falls if he or she loses balance and can't regain it. From the point of view of the laws of biomechanics, this happens when the projection of the center of gravity extends beyond the area of support. Let's look at the techniques that ensure that your opponent will fall that are most often encountered in fighting.

In the first technique, you try to break a person's balance by forcing him or her to step on the foot that he or she can't use. This is easy to try out in practice. Walk up to your partner from behind, bend your arms at the elbows, push your palms into the area around your partner's shoulder blades, and forcefully shove him or her forward as you straighten your arms. Your partner will be forced to take a step forward (perhaps several, depending on the force of the push) to prevent falling, to bring their area of support under the shifting general center of gravity.

Now, do the same thing, asking someone to hold your partner's feet as he or she is pushed, or place some obstacle, for example a gymnastics bench, in front of your partner. This time, because your partner is unable to budge, he or she will lose balance and will be forced to execute a forward break-falling technique. A vivid illustration of this technique in practice is the body drop (tai-otoshi).

Let's look at the second mechanism for causing a person to fall. In this technique, you break a person's balance who, in order to regain his or her balance, must stand on the leg that he or she can't use. Ask your partner to bend his left leg at the knee and balance on his right leg. Shove your partner in the right shoulder. In order to regain balance and not fall, your partner will be forced to put down his left foot, bringing the area of support to the now-shifted center of gravity.

If you don't allow your partner to straighten his leg and put it down, so as to avoid falling (for example, by holding your shin against your partner's hip), then a strong push will force him to fall. Hooks, foot sweeps, and leg-hold throws are based on this principle.

Jigoro Kano's rational, one might say materialistic, approach to the problem of *tanden*, the focusing of bioenergy, whose concentration—according to the traditional approach of Eastern martial arts adherents—makes it possible to achieve outstanding results, commands respect. Judo's founder saw tanden above all as the human body's center of gravity. He studied the laws of mechanics and the theory of balance, as applied to special acrobatics, meticulously. In judo, *kuzushi* (breaking balance) has been developed in great detail. The correct execution of kuzushi is half of judo, since a person standing firmly on his feet cannot be thrown.

The meaning behind the Kodokan's motto—"The Most Efficient Application of Strength," as Jigoro Kano put it—consists of the following. Assume that a person's strength is measured in some sort of units. An opponent's strength is ten, yours is seven. If your opponent pushes you with all his might, you won't be able remain standing, even if you resist with all your might. You'll either fall or step back. This is opposing strength with strength. But if you give way to the extent that you are pushed, maintaining your balance and withdrawing your body, your opponent will stagger forward and lose balance. At that moment, weakened by this awkward position, your opponent is very vulnerable. You, on the other hand, by maintaining your balance, can use all seven units of your strength, to score a victory.

"Give way in order to conquer." The highest degree of judo mastery is the ability to give way in the name of victory. Let's illustrate this tenet with the following example. Imagine you are a door and that you are locked shut; your opponent, however, is determined to break you open with his shoulder. If your opponent is big and strong enough and rams through the door (that is, you) from a running start, he will achieve his aim. Now let's consider a different turn of events. Instead of digging in your heels and resisting your opponent's onslaught, you time it so that when your opponent is just about to hit the door, you unlatch it. Then, not meeting any resistance and unable to stop, your opponent bursts through the wide open door, losing balance and falling. If at this time you raise the threshold slightly, "stick out your heel," so that he trips (if we're going to fantasize, let's do it right), then victory will be unconditional. Minimum effort, maximum effect.

Similarly, you can play with the lock when the door opens outward and your opponent pulls the door (that is, you) open. As soon as your opponent tries to jerk the handle, thinking he is going to break down the locked door, the lock is opened and he is sure to lose balance. If at this time we are able to take the handle off the door, as it were, then that person, who was counting on brute strength but met no resistance while groping with the void, will surely fall on his back.

Throwing Techniques (Nage-Waza)

Shoulder Throw (Seoi-Nage)

There are several variations of this technique. The following ones are encountered most frequently in competitive practice.

Variation 1. Morote-Seoi-Nage

1. Tori grab the opposite sleeve and lapel.
2. Pull the opponent off balance.
3. Continuing to pull uke forward and up, force uke to rise up on balls of feet.
4. Turn back to uke, squat down slightly, and bend forward, lifting uke off the mat, removing his support.
5. Straightening legs and shoving uke's pelvis with hips, throw the opponent over your body.

See Figure 1 on next page.

Variation 2. Morote-Seoi-Nage

This differs from the first in that, in order to carry out the attack, you grab the same collar of uke's jacket.

1. Tori grab opposite sleeve and same lapel.
2. Pull your opponent off balance.

Figure 1.
Morote-seoi-nage

3. Continuing to pull uke forward and up, force uke to rise up on the balls of his feet.

4. Turn your back to uke, squat down slightly, and bend forward, lifting uke off the mat, removing his support.

5. Straightening your legs and shoving uke's pelvis with your hips, throw uke over your body.

Variation 3. Ippon-Seoi-Nage

Just as with the previous variations, you must grab the opponent's opposite sleeve from below, between the elbow and shoulder joints. The other hand, after unbalancing the opponent and at the moment when tori turns his back, with a motion from the armpit of the attacked arm, uses the same shoulder as an extra point of support. Then, straightening your knees and shoving uke's pelvis with your hips, throw uke over your body.

Variation 4. Two-Sleeve Shoulder Throw

1. Tori grab the opposite sleeves of your opponent's jacket from below, close to the hands.
2. Hold your opponent's arms without letting him go.
3. When your opponent tries to break free and starts to lift his hands, use his effort and, with a thrust, continue the movement of his arms as high as possible over his head, while squatting slightly and turning your back to your opponent.
4. Continuing the upward and forward motion, throw your opponent on his back.

Variation 5. Kneeling Shoulder Throw

1. Tori grab opposite sleeve and opposite (same) lapel.
2. Pull opponent forward off balance.
3. Continuing to pull uke forward and upward, forcing your opponent to rise up on the balls of his feet.
4. Turn your back to uke and quickly drop to your knees as close to the opponent as possible.
5. Continuing to draw your opponent forward and down, throw him over your body.

Note the following favorable conditions for shoulder throw techniques:

1. The opponent moves forward in an attack, making it easier to unbalance him. The opponent bends forward, making it easier to unbalance him by drawing him forward.
2. The opponent increases the pressure by trying to get away, making it easier to pull him forward off balance.
3. The opponent, while not grabbed, tries to grab, which provides an opportunity to grab the attacking hand and reverse the attack.
4. After warding off an attack, the opponent returns to the starting position, which also presents an opportunity to reverse the attack and execute a shoulder throw.

The most effective methods are various tactical ones for preparing a shoulder throw. One method is to threaten your opponent with an attack. This method of tactical preparation involves the use of a favorable dynamic situation for executing a throw, which arises as a result of uke's defensive actions. These defensive actions can be brought about by the beginning of an attack using one of the following techniques:

1. Major outer drop
2. Major inner reaping
3. Minor inner hook
4. Advancing foot sweep
5. Knee sweep
6. Body drop
7. Shoulder throw in opposite direction

(see Figure 2)

The uke's defensive actions against the shoulder throw (seoi-nage) may create a favorable dynamic situation for carrying out an attack using techniques such as

1. Minor inner hook
2. Major outer reaping
3. Major inner reaping
4. Shoulder throw with change in direction of attack (in opposite direction relative to beginning)
5. Shoulder throw with changing level of attack (dropping to knees)

(see Figure 3)

Figure 2. Technical-tactical set with one-arm
shoulder throw as the final technique

Figure 3. Technical-tactical set with one-arm
shoulder throw as combination set-up technique

Body Drop (Tai-Otoshi)

Despite its name, in the Japanese classification system, the body drop is one of the throws that are executed with the hands (te-waza). Indeed, the role of the attacking leg is simply to create an obstacle that keeps the opponent from regaining balance. The act itself of unbalancing, which forces the uke to fall, is executed with the hands (undoubtedly other muscle groups are also at work). Why does uke fall? The biomechanical mechanism is approximately the following. Imagine that you are walking in the forest carrying a heavy backpack. It's getting dark, and on the path at knee level there is a fallen tree. If you don't notice it in time, you'll bump into it and stumble. The backpack, through inertia, will continue its forward movement, while the body bends forward. The only way to regain your balance is by taking a step forward; but the obstacle is in your way, and so you fall forward.

On the mat, tori's blocking leg is like the fallen tree, while the heavy backpack, with its great inertia, represents the efforts of tori's arms.

1. Tori grab the opposite collar and opposite sleeve under the elbow. This is a standard attack grab.

2. Stepping aside, turn your side to your opponent, bend your arms, and pull your opponent off balance, forcing him or her to rise up on the balls of his feet.

3. At the same time, continuing to turn your back to your opponent and squatting slightly on far leg, block both of uke's legs with straightened leg, preventing him or her from stepping forward.

4. Continuing to turn your torso and drawing your arms forward, throw your opponent over your blocking leg.

The following may serve as tactical preparation for applying the body drop:

1. Major inner reaping
2. Advancing foot sweep
3. Minor inner sweep
4. Outer leg hook
5. Inner thigh reaping
6. Hip throw
7. Sweeping drawing ankle

Figure 4. Body drop (tai-otoshi)

Figure 5. Technical-tactical set with body drop as the final technique

When your opponent successfully defends an attack, the beginning of a body drop attack can, in turn, create a favorable situation for continuing an attack by transitioning to:

1. Shoulder throw
2. Major outer reaping
3. Heel sweep
4. Inside sweep
5. Major inner reaping
6. Body drop (in a repeat attack)

Figure 6. Technical-tactical set with body drop as combination set-up technique.

Major Outer Reaping (O-Soto-Gari)

Tori's task is to throw the opponent off balance backwards and not allow uke to regain balance by stepping back. Grab the opposite sleeve and opposite lapel or collar. The final phase of the attack is sweeping away the opponent's support leg.

The projection of the general center of gravity extends beyond the support area, which doesn't move. Then the support area is eliminated, a take-down occurs.

Figure 7. Major outer reaping
(o-soto-gari)

A situation favorable for a major outer reaping can be set up by the following:

1. Advancing foot sweep
2. Heel sweep
3. Hip throw
4. Body drop
5. Two-arm throw
6. Sweeping drawing ankle

Figure 8. Technical-tactical set with major outer reaping throw as the final combination technique

If your opponent is able to defend against your attack, the major outer reaping can, in turn, create a favorable situation for continuing an attack by the following:

1. Heel sweep
2. Hip throw
3. Circle throw
4. Two-arm throw
5. Shoulder throw
6. Inner thigh reaping
7. Under-the-shoulder throw
8. Sweeping drawing ankle
9. Major outer drop

If the attacking leg doesn't lose contact with the mat and serves as an obstacle, preventing your opponent from regaining his balance by repositioning his legs, you can throw your opponent mainly with arm and torso movements. In this case, we are dealing with a major outer drop throw technique (o-soto-otoshi).

Figure 9. Technical-tactical set with major outer reaping as the combination set-up technique.

Major Inner Reaping (O-Uchi-Gari)

When this technique is executed correctly, the opponent falls, since after being pushed off balance he can't regain his balance while standing on the attacked leg, which is under tori's complete control.

1. Tori grab the opposite sleeve from below around the elbow and the opposite lapel (or collar) of your opponent's jacket.

2. Determine (or create) the moment when the opponent's forward leg is the same side as the grabbed collar.

3. With the opposite inside shin, block the opponent's forward leg (keeping close contact using the bend in the back of the knees).

4. Sweep the blocked leg in toward your body while thrusting your hands out and bending your body in the direction of the attacked leg, throwing your opponent on his back.

Figure 10. Major inner reaping (o-uchi-gari)

The beginning of a major inner reaping attack can, in turn, cause defensive reactions in uke that allow you to complete the attack using the following

1. Inside sweep
2. Body drop
3. Shoulder throw
4. Circle throw
5. Inner thigh reaping
6. Two-hand throw
7. Ankle sweeps

Figure 11. Technical-tactical set with major inner reaping as the combination set-up technique

A favorable situation for completing an attack with this technique arises after uke's defensive actions, caused by the real threat of the first phase of the attack, which may include the following:

1. Two-hand throw
2. Inner thigh reaping
3. Body drop
4. Shoulder throw
5. Circle throw
6. Hip throw
7. Sweeping drawing ankle
8. Inside sweep

Figure 12. Technical- tactical set with major inner reaping as the final combination technique

One-Leg or Sweeping Hip Throw (Harai-Goshi)

1. Tori grab the opposite sleeve (around the elbow) and the opposite lapel (collar, jacket on the back).

2. Pull your opponent off balance while transferring your weight to the forward leg.

3. Turn your back to the opponent

4. While continuing to extend your arms outward, with a backward sweeping motion of the straightened leg, sweep away the opponent's supporting leg.

5. Uke's fall occurs due to the forward displacement of the general center of gravity (as a result of tori's arm and torso movement).

Figure 13. Sweeping hip throw (harai-goshi)

JUDO

A favorable situation for executing the throw may be set up by the following:

1. Advancing foot sweep
2. Heel sweep
3. Hip throw
4. Major outer drop
5. Sweeping drawing ankle
6. Major inner reaping
7. Minor inner sweep

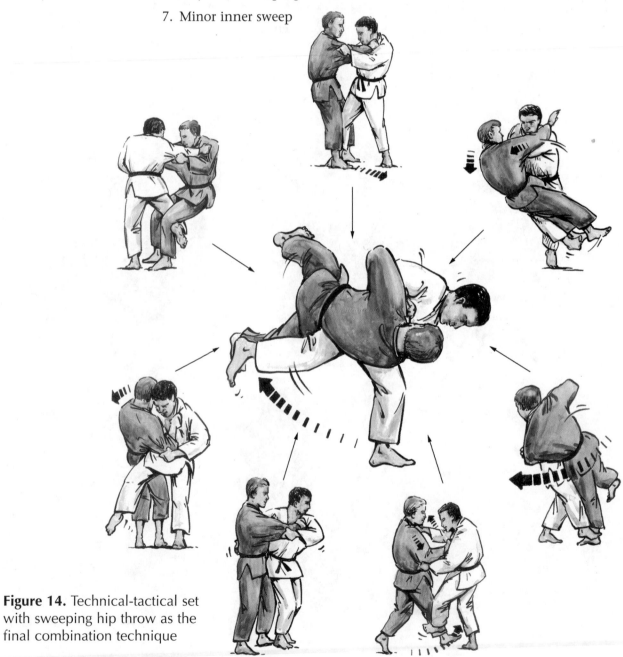

Figure 14. Technical-tactical set with sweeping hip throw as the final combination technique

If the opponent is able to defend against the attack, the sweeping hip throw can, in turn, create a favorable situation for continuing the attack using the following techniques:

1. Heel sweep
2. Hip throw
3. Major inner reaping
4. Major outer reaping
5. Knee wheel
6. Lifting pulling ankle sweep

Figure 15. Technical-tactical set with sweeping hip throw as the combination set-up technique

Inner Thigh Throw (Uchi-Mata)

When this technique is used, your opponent is deprived of his support area due to the powerful leg sweep from back to front, while the arms are pulled forward and down; by actively bending and turning his body in the direction of his support leg, tori sweeps his opponent's leg from inside (around the inner upper thigh).

There are a variety of attack grabs: opposite sleeve and opposite lapel, opposite sleeve and same lapel, opposite sleeve and collar, opposite sleeve and back of jacket.

1. Decide on an attack grab.
2. Pull the opponent forward off balance, forcing uke to rise up on the balls of his feet.
3. While continuing the upward motion of your arms, turn your back to uke so that your support leg is in line with uke's legs.
4. With a sweep of your free leg, shove the opponent's opposite hip from inside, depriving him of support.
5. Turning your torso in the direction of your support leg, throw the opponent on his back.

Figure 16. Inner thigh throw (uchi-mata)

There is a variation of this technique whereby uke, after tori sweeps with his leg, does not lose complete contact·with the mat and hops on his support leg in an attempt not to fall. In this case, tori may hop once (or several times), bringing his center of gravity under uke, while continuing the forward movement of his arms and turning his torso in the direction of his support leg. This variation is called ken-ken-uchi-mata.

A favorable situation for completing the inner thigh throw attack can be artificially created by the threat of the following:

1. Body drop
2. Two-hand sweep
3. Advancing foot sweep

4. Minor inner sweep
5. Major outer drop
6. Major inner reaping

Figure 17. Technical-tactical set with inner thigh throw as the final combination technique

Uke's defensive actions against the inner thigh throw can, in turn, be used for completing the attack with the following techniques:

1. Minor inner sweep
2. Heel sweep
3. Major inner reaping
4. Body drop
5. Circle throw
6. Corner reversal

Figure 18. Technical-tactical set with inner thigh throw as the combination set-up technique

Circle Throw (Tomoe-Nage)

This is the most eye-catching technique in the judo arsenal. The main components of the move that make this technique so appealing are when the opponent is completely lifted off the mat, flips in the air, and strikes the mat powerfully when landing (almost always on his back when done right). Grab the jacket sleeve from below, close to the shoulder joints or both lapels. (You can also do an asymmetrical grab: sleeve-lapel.)

In order to execute this technique successfully, tori must force the opponent to move forward so as to minimize his effort in making the throw.

1. Tori begin moving back, luring your rival with you.
2. Grabbing downward with both arms, force your opponent to bend, causing him to react and straighten up.
3. When uke straightens up, take a step forward and lower yourself as close as possible to his center of gravity, while thrusting your half-bent leg into his stomach.
4. Continuing to pull your arms in and back, straighten your leg, and lift your opponent off the mat.
5. Continuing to pull his arms, throw him over your head.
6. Fall back and come out on top.

(See Figure 19)

After the attack has begun, a favorable situation for executing the circle throw may arise by executing the following:

1. Advancing foot sweep
2. Heel sweep
3. Inner reaping when uke's defensive reaction creates more free space between the two judoka.

The circle throw may be executed with a unilateral grab.

1. Tori grabs the inside sleeve of the jacket near the elbow and the outside lapel near the collarbone.
2. Stepping toward the grabbed sleeve, tori ends up next to uke.
3. Bending down on the near leg, the other foot thrusts into uke's lower abdomen.

4. Continuing the inward arm movement, tori falls on his back and quickly straightens his leg, lifting uke off the mat.

5. Tori throws uke over his head.

6. Tori does a reverse somersault and comes out on top.

Figure 19. Circle throw (tomoe-nage).

Corner Reversal (Sumi-Gaeshi)

This throw differs from the previous one in that tori doesn't thrust the foot of his straightened leg into uke's abdomen so as to throw him overhead, but bends his leg at the knee and slips his lower leg between uke's legs.

In order to complete this technique successfully, you must bend the arms more at the elbow. This is necessary so that uke's head is lower than his pelvis during the throw.

The most effective grab for this throw is to grab uke's belt from behind and in a downward motion with one hand.

Figure 20. Corner reversal (sumi-gaeshi)

Shoulder Wheel "The Mill" (Kata-Guruma)

1. Tori grabs the inside lapel or sleeve of uke's jacket.
2. Tori pulls uke inward, unbalancing him.
3. Tori turns his side to uke, bends down, and moves in as close as possible to the projection of uke's center of gravity, and with his free arm grabs the outside thigh from inside. Continuing to pull in his arms, he straightens up, forcing uke off the mat.
4. When uke is on tori's shoulders, tori turns his torso toward uke's head and throws him down on his back in front of tori, directing uke's head underneath his body.

(See Figure 21)

One variation of this technique is called the "knee wheel," in which tori, after grabbing and throwing uke off balance, reaches for the same thigh from inside with his free hand and drops to his knees. Then, using his arms to lower uke's head and lift his legs, tori throws uke on his back.

Figure 21. Shoulder wheel "the mill" (kata-guruma)

Outer Wraparound (Soto-Maki-Komi)

This technique is executed solely through tori's falling.

1. Tori grabs the opposite sleeve of uke's jacket near the elbow (or opposite lapel).

2. Tori pushes uke off balance.

3. Tori raises his free hand and turns his side to uke. Continuing his forward movement, tori puts his free hand over uke's head and squeezes the previously grabbed hand in his armpit. Continuing to turn, he falls into a somersault and throws his opponent over his back.

Figure 22. Outer wraparound (soto-maki-komi).

Hand Wheel (Te-Guruma)

This technique involves full contact with uke. The starting distance is for completing the attack up close. Possible grab variations: grab opposite thigh from the outside and grab the back of the jacket with opposite hand (or from under the opposite hand, or over the opposite hand).

The most important part of executing this technique is to step toward the opponent as close to his center of gravity as possible and lift him off the mat using your torso. Uke is left without a support, and tori turns him upside down and throws him on his back.

Figure 23. Side wheel (te-guruma)

Scoop Throw (Sukui-Nage)

This technique involves full contact with uke. The start distance is for completing the attack up close. Possible grab variations: same thigh from inside and back of jacket with opposite hand (or from under the opposite hand, or over the opposite hand).

The most important thing about executing this technique is to step toward your opponent as close to his center of gravity as possible and use your torso to lift your opponent off the mat. Uke is left without a support, and tori turns uke upside down and throws him on his back.

Figure 24. Scoop throw (sukui-nage)

Rear Hip Throw (Ushiro-Goshi)

The universal counter technique when tori turns his back toward uke. When any attempt is made at carrying out attack actions associated with tori's turning his back to his opponent (in forward throws), uke should do the following:

1. Meet tori's back and hips with his body.
2. Try to maintain his balance, countering tori's arms by leaning his torso back.
3. Tightly embrace tori's entire torso, bend his near leg (at the pelvis and knee), and, straightening up on his support leg, throw tori down with his hip up.
4. Depriving him of support and contact with the mat, he throws his opponent on his back.

Figure 25. Rear hip throw (Ushiro-Goshi)

Ground-Fighting Techniques (Ne-Waza)

Judo's technical arsenal on the ground is extraordinarily varied. Experience has shown that fighting in a standing position will lead to a clean victory only through throws. Ground fighting provides an opportunity to win straight out through three fundamentally different methods: holds, joint locking, and choking techniques.

A brief historical digression. The number of jujitsu schools and, most importantly, teaching methods and practical techniques in Japan at the end of the nineteenth century started to exceed reasonable boundaries. In 1886, the authorities came to the conclusion that the prevailing situation should be put in order and the most important direction for jujitsu's growth be determined. The decision was made to hold a meeting between the self-proclaimed leading schools. The goal was specific—to choose the single most effective system and teach according to that system. By decree of the chief of the Imperial Police directive, command competitions were held between fifteen masters from each side. The outcome of the match settled the matter. In thirteen meetings the students of Jigoro Kano won, with two matches ending in a tie.

It should be noted that the affair didn't pass without some tactical cunning on the part of judo's creator. Knowing that his rivals were better at ground fighting, he insisted that the competition be conducted according to rules that limited the use of such techniques. Preference was given to standing fighting, where the students of the Kodokan were clearly stronger. Later, this measure (which undoubtedly played a positive role in judo's fate) had negative consequences. The insufficient attention that was devoted to ground-fighting techniques was evident in the first meetings with Soviet judoka—representatives of the sambo school—which had highly developed armlock techniques.

But there's a reason why the Japanese are masters at borrowing the experience of other countries and peoples, each time adding something new with Japan's own specific national coloring. This process cannot properly be called blind copying. And this time was no exception—today there is no trace of the former lag among Japanese judoka in this area of technique.

Hold-Down Techniques (Osaekomi-Waza)

A hold-down in judo is a position in which your opponent is held in place from above, facing you on his back, with tori pressing his chest or side against uke.

Hold-downs are a powerful way of winning in ground fighting. A clean victory is awarded for a hold-down of 25 seconds. A hold-down of 10 to 14 seconds is counted as "koka," 15 to 19 seconds as "yuko," and 20 to 24 seconds as "waza-ari."

Hold-downs are subdivided into side holds, top holds, vertical holds, cross holds, and upper holds. The most commonly encountered hold-downs in competition are listed below.

Side Holds

Scarf Hold (Kesa-Gatame)

Uke is on his back. Tori sits to the side, the leg closest to uke is directed toward his head. From the side, tori presses down on uke's chest. He grabs uke's inside hand, slips his second hand under the back of uke's head, and presses his head in to his own body. It is important that uke not touch the mat with the back of his head (so as not to have an additional support point).

Figure 26. Scarf hold
(kesa-gatame)

Side Body Hold (Kashira-Gatame)

Uke is on his back. Tori sits beside him with the leg closest to uke directed toward his head. Tori presses his side against uke's chest and grabs uke's collar from the far armpit with both hands. With his near hand tori controls the opponent's other arm (by grabbing the back of his jacket close to the collar).

Figure 27. Side body hold
(kashira-gatame)

Shoulder Hold (Kata-Gatame)

Uke is on his back. Tori sits beside him with leg closest to uke directed toward his head. Tori presses on uke's chest with his side and presses uke's near arm with the back of his head to the same shoulder. He slips his other hand behind uke's head and presses his head up to his own body. He joins the two hands in a firm grab. It is important that uke not touch the mat with the back of his head (so as not to have an extra support point).

Figure 28. Shoulder hold (kata-gatame)

Upper Holds

Upper Four-Quarter Hold (Kami-Shiho-Gatame)

Tori is situated above uke's head. He slips both hands under uke's back while squeezing uke's hands under the arms, grabs uke's belt, and establishes complete control over uke.

(See Figure 29.)

Broken Upper Four-Quarter Hold (Kuzure-Kami-Shiho-Gatame)

Tori is situated above uke's head. He presses uke's arms to his torso and, at the same time, grabs uke's belt from behind. With the armpit of his second arm, he control uke's other arm and grabs the collar of his jacket. He has complete control over uke.

(See Figure 30.)

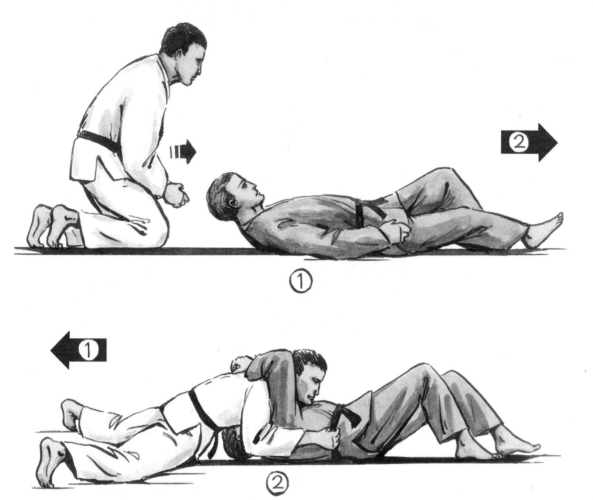

Figure 29. Upper four-quarter
hold (kami-shiho-gatame)

Figure 30. Broken upper four-quarter hold
(kuzure-kami-shiho-gatame)

Upper Four-Quarter Hold (Ura-Shiho-Gatame)

Tori is situated above uke's head. He slips one hand under uke's back and grabs his belt, while squeezing uke's outside hand with his armpit. He controls uke, preventing him from turning over on his stomach.

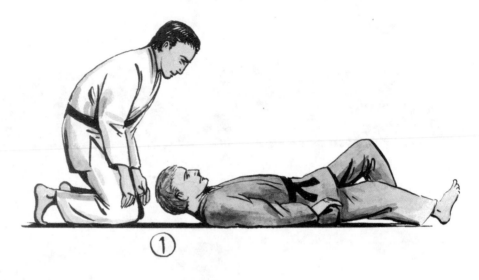

①

Figure 31. Upper four-quarter hold (ura-shiho-gatame)

②

Cross Holds

Broken Side-Locking Four-Quarter Hold (Kuzure-Yoko-Shiho-Gatame)

Uke is on his back. Tori is on top at a 90 degree angle. Tori grabs uke's far (same) arm and slips his other arm between uke's legs and tries to grip uke's belt from behind. He controls uke, preventing him from turning over on his stomach.

Figure 32. Broken side-locking four-quarter hold
(kuzure-yoko-shiho-gatame)

Chest Hold (Mune-Gatame)

Uke is on his back. Tori is on top at a 90 degree angle. Tori grabs uke's far arm with both hands. He controls uke, preventing him from turning over on his stomach.

Figure 33. Chest hold (mune-gatame)

JUDO

Side-Locking Four-Quarter Hold (Yoko-Shiho-Gatame)

Uke is on his back. Tori is on top at a 90 degree angle. Tori grabs uke's head, sliding his other hand between uke's legs and trying to grab his belt from behind. He controls uke, not allowing him to turn over on his stomach.

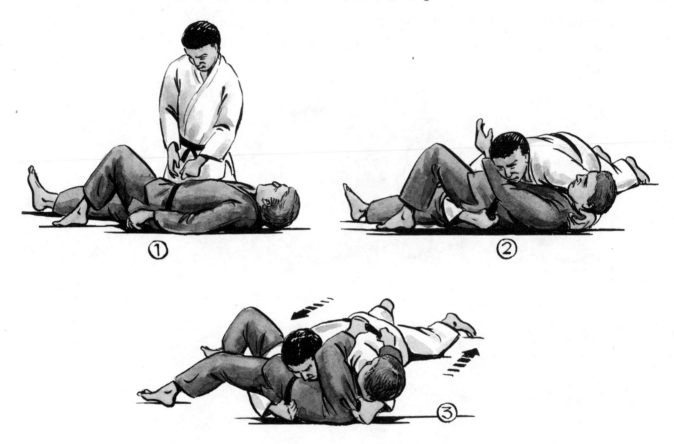

Figure 34. Side-locking four-quarter hold (yoko-shiho-gatame)

Vertical Holds with Various Grips

Vertical Four-Quarter Hold (Tate-Sankaku-Gatame)

Uke is on his back. Tori straddles him on top (facing him). The legs play an important role. Squeezing his thighs, tori makes it more difficult for uke to get out of the hold. He grips uke's arm and head, pressing firmly against uke's chest. He controls uke, preventing him from turning over on his stomach.

Figure 35. Variation of vertical four-quarter hold (tate-sankaku-gatame)

Straight Locking Four-Quarter Hold (Tate-Shiho-Gatame)

Uke is on his back. Tori straddles him on top (facing him). The legs play an important role. Squeezing his thighs, tori makes it more difficult for uke to get out of the hold. He grabs uke's head with one hand. With this hold, tori leans on the mat with his free hand, using it as an extra support. Pressing tightly against uke's chest, tori controls uke, not allowing him to turn over on his stomach.

Figure 36. Variation of vertical four-quarter hold (tate-shiho-gatame).

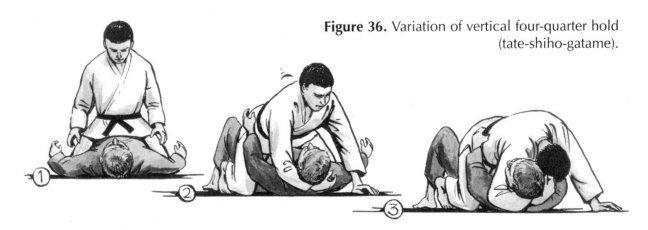

During training, serious attention should be paid to hold escape techniques. There are several variations for getting out of side hold-downs:

1. Intertwine your legs with uke's nearest leg (in this case, the hold time ends in accordance with the rules).

2. Wrapping your arms around your opponent's torso and bending at the waist, shove your opponent in the direction of your head and drag him over your chest.

3. Sharply raising and letting down your straightened legs, switch to a sitting position and move to a hold.

4. Jerking the grabbed hand toward your body while pushing away your opponent's torso, turn over on your stomach.

When getting out of an upper, vertical, or cross hold, your main task is to create a gap, even a slight one, between yourself and your opponent, to make it possible to turn over on your stomach. This is accomplished by pushing your opponent away by any allowable methods. Therefore, an important part of executing a hold is the tight contact between tori's body and uke.

Training Exercises for Mastering Hold Escape Techniques

Uke gives tori the chance to grab him comfortably. After the command "Hajime!" is given, uke must get out of the hold as quickly as possible.

The time to complete the task should vary from 10 to 25 seconds, in accordance with the rules of the match. The spatial component plays an additional role—the distance from the edge of the mat varies. Leaving the boundaries of the mat results in the end of the hold.

Armlock (Pain-Causing) Techniques (Kansetsu-Waza)

The name of this group of techniques speaks for itself. The opponent is forced to stop resisting and surrender because of increasing pain in the elbow joint. According to competition rules, only elbow joint techniques are allowed in judo.

There are two different mechanisms for causing pain: levers (straight arms) and knots. A lever is a technical move meant to hyperextend the joint, an effort aimed at an unnatural bending of the elbow. Uke's arm can hyperextend across the thigh, chest, or forearm.

The knot involves turning a bent arm (at an angle of no less than 90 degree).

Repeated slapping of the hand or foot on the mat (or on one's own body or that of your opponent, or the cry "Give" or "Maita"—"I give up"—serves as a signal that no further resistance is possible. Other exclamations do not signal a surrender.

In children's competition, in order to avoid injury, the very fact that a leg has been straightened or an armlock technique has been executed serves as a sign of a clean victory.

Straight Arm Side Hold (Kesa-Garami)

This armlock technique is a convenient place to introduce beginners to this group of judo techniques. In the initial position, tori executes a side hold, grabbing uke's near arm and head. Uke tries to get out of the hold and extricates his seized arm. Tori grabs uke's near wrist and brings his near thigh up to uke's elbow. Pressing down with his torso on uke's upper body and with his hand on the seized forearm, tori causes pain in the elbow joint by hyperextending it. To increase the effect, tori can slightly raise up the thigh that was placed under the elbow.

Figure 37. Straight arm side hold (kesa-garami)

If uke, in an attempt to defend himself, won't let his arm be straightened, bends it, and turns the palm up, tori can, by raising the knee of the bent near leg, grab the opponent's forearm by bending his knee and move his torso forward. The elbow will twist ("the knot").

Cross Armlock (Ude-Hishigi-Juji-Gatame)

The cross armlock technique in its various forms is responsible for most clean victories in competition. The most important part of this armlock technique is to quickly take up the starting position, when uke has no chance to maneuver, is under tori's complete control, and is left only to defend himself. The starting position for carrying out the final phase of this technique is as follows:

1. Uke is lying on his back.

2. Tori sits as close as possible (at about a 90 degree angle) and, grabbing the near arm below the elbow, squeezes the arms with both thighs and places his legs on uke's chest.

3. Tori straightens the seized arm.

4. Bending the elbow joint beyond its natural range, tori causes sharp pain and forces his opponent to give in.

Let's look at ways of taking up a position when you can execute this armlock technique.

Figure 38. Cross armlock
(ude-hishigi-juji-gatame)

Method 1. Othen-Garami

Uke is lying on his stomach; tori is on top. Tori grabs uke's belt with both hands and lifts him up, forcing him on all fours. Tori grabs uke's same arm from under the shoulder near the elbow, places the opposite leg across uke's head, and grips his head in the back of his knee. Tori rolls forward, helping himself with a sweep of his leg, thereby putting pressure on uke's head, and ends at the starting position as described above.

Figure 39. Othen-garami

JUDO

Method 2. Othen-Garami

Uke is lying on his stomach; tori is on top. Tori grabs uke's belt with both hands and lifts him, forcing him on all fours. Tori grabs uke's outside arm from under the shoulder near the elbow, transfers the opposite leg across uke's head, and sits back, turning the opponent on his back. He ends at the starting position as described above.

Method 3. Kami-Ude-Hishigi-Juji-Gatame

Tori is executing a hold-down from on top. Uke, trying to get out of the hold, pushes tori away, straightening his arms. Tori grabs his arms and places his inside leg across uke's head. He squeezes the seized arm, pressing his thighs tightly and crossing his lower legs. Then, he executes an armlock technique—straight arm.

Figure 40. Kami-ude-hishigi-juji-gatame

It is rather difficult to force your opponent to straighten his arm. In self-defense, your opponent will clasp his hands, grab his jacket or tori's jacket, and do whatever he can so as not to give up his arm. The most important aspects to pay attention to in order to break your opponent's resistance, using minimum effort for maximum effect, are the following:

1. Place your hands as close as possible to uke's wrist, thereby increasing the leverage.

2. Use your back muscles.

3. Work your arms away from your body so that your opponent cannot turn over on his stomach.

Arm Crush (Ude-Hishigi)

If uke has clasped his hands tightly, resists stubbornly, and won't let tori straighten his near arm, another variation of this technique involving the far elbow can be applied. In the initial position, tori sits to uke's right, having grabbed his near arm and tried to straighten it. For this maneuver, tori must:

1. Slip his left forearm under his opponent's far forearm.
2. Bring uke's arm closer to his body by pressing down on uke's elbow with his right hand.
3. Secure uke's hand between uke's head and left shoulder.
4. Execute the armlock technique by pressing with both forearms on the straightened arm near the elbow.

Figure 41. Ude-hishigi

Straight Arm with Tori Below

In the initial position, tori is on his back. Uke tries to move to a hold from the direction of his legs.

1. Tori grabs uke's inside sleeve.
2. At the same time, he grabs the inside leg from inside.
3. Tori turns his head in the direction of the seized leg.
4. He transfers the seized hand on the outside shoulder.
5. With a sweep of his leg, tori grabs uke's head and, shoving him away from his body, ends at the start position for executing the udi-hishigi-juji-gatame armlock technique.

(See Figure 42)

JUDO

Just as in standing fighting, judoka who are able to switch from one technique to another depending on how the situation unfolds have an advantage. In ground fighting this takes on added significance, since on the ground a clean victory is possible through three methods: hold-down, armlock, or choking techniques. By using the defensive actions of uke, who has been deprived of the chance to maneuver freely, in ground fighting, as opposed to standing fighting, tori can distract his opponent's attention by backing him into a pre-prepared trap from the three different forms of ground fighting.

Figure 42. Straight arm with tori below

Choke Techniques (Shime-Waza)

Choke techniques are a powerful method for achieving a clean victory in judo. A choke technique is an action in the opponent's neck area designed to neutralize his defense capabilities by bringing about a state of asphyxia.

Two different physiological mechanisms are involved in choking: respiratory choking, in which the windpipe is squeezed and passage to the lungs is blocked, and the so-called "blood" choke, in which blood vessels in the neck are squeezed and oxygen-rich blood flow to the brain is cut off. A choke technique carried out to completion can cause a loss of consciousness through one of the following events:

1. Hypoxemia: a decrease in oxygen content in blood that supplies the brain as a result of excessive squeezing of the carotid arteries.

2. Hypercapnia: an increase in carbon dioxide (CO_2) and H_2CO_3 in blood in the brain as a result of excessive squeezing of the jugular and other surface veins. Edema of the brain sets in.

3. A reflex response as a result of the mechanical pressure on the carotid sinuses of the carotid arteries.

4. A reflex response to pressure of the vagus.

5. A reflex of the proprioceptors of the neck muscles.

From the point of view of motion biomechanics, chokes are carried out in two ways: squeezing and suffocation. Squeezing is achieved by applying pressure on the neck with parts of the body (hands, forearms). Suffocation is achieved by using the jacket (lapels).

Choke Techniques with Tori and Uke Facing Each Other

Gyaku-Juji-Jime

Uke is on his back; tori executes a vertical hold-down. Uke is able to end the hold through defensive moves (for example, tori's leg is entangled).

Tori, maintaining the top position, slips his crossed hands under the outside lapels of uke's jacket as close to the neck as possible, practically touching the ears with his index fingers (palms are turned toward tori). Spreading his elbows apart and drawing the opponent in toward his body and turning his

JUDO

palms out, tori presses down on the sides of the opponent's neck with the back of his hands and chokes him.

Figure 43. Choke technique gyaku-juji-jime

Nami-Juji-Jime

Uke is on his back; tori executes a vertical hold. Uke is able to end the hold through defensive moves (for example, tori's leg is entangled).

Tori, maintaining the top position, grabs the outside lapel of uke's jacket as close to the neck as possible, practically touching the ears with his pinky fingers (palms are turned downward toward uke). Spreading his elbows apart, drawing his opponent in toward his body, and bringing his palms closer together, tori presses down on his opponent's neck with the back of his hands and executes a choke.

Figure 44. Choke technique nami-juji-jime

JUDO

Kata-Juji-Jime

Uke is on his back; tori executes a vertical hold. Uke is able to stop the hold through defensive moves (for example, tori's leg is entangled).

Tori, maintaining the top position, slips his crossed hands under the outside lapel of uke's jacket as close to the neck as possible, practically touching his ears with his fingers (the base of one palm is turned toward tori, the other toward uke). Spreading the elbows apart and pulling the lower lapel toward his body, tori presses down on the side of the neck with his forearm, which is on top, and executes the choke.

Figure 45. Choke technique kata-juji-jime

Choke Techniques with Tori Behind Uke

Ushiro-Jime

Uke is on his stomach; tori is on top.

Tori lifts uke's head slightly with one arm, steadying the forehead only, and slips his second hand under uke's chin. He clasps his hands and, using his chest to stabilize the back of the opponent's head, executes a choke, pressing down on the opponent's neck with his forearm.

Figure 46. Choke technique ushiro-jime

Kata-Ha-Jime

Uke is on his stomach; tori is on top.

Tori slips his hand under uke's chin and grabs the outside lapel of his jacket. He puts his other hand on the back of uke's head from under the opponent's outside armpit. Pressing down on the opponent's neck, he executes the choke with a counter motion of his forearm.

Figure 47. Choke technique kata-ha-jime.

Hadaka-Jime

Uke is on his stomach; tori is on top.

Tori slips his hand under uke's chin and grabs his elbow with his other hand. The palm of his second hand is placed on the back of uke's head. With a counter motion of his forearms, he presses down on the opponent's neck and chokes him.

Figure 48. Choke technique hadaka-jime

Sode-Guruma

Uke is on his stomach; tori is on top or to the side.

Tori slips his hand under uke's chin and grabs his outside lapel (four fingers under the jacket), puts his other hand on the back of uke's head, and grabs the same lapel (thumb under jacket). Crossing his forearms, he presses down on the opponent's neck and chokes him.

To ensure an effective attack, the thumb of the hand under the chin must touch the pinky finger of the other hand at the spot where the hand grabs.

Figure 49. Choke technique sode-guruma.

Running Opposite Lapel

The most effective choke technique, the one that is responsible for the most clean victories in competition, is known as "running opposite lapel."

In the initial position, uke is on his stomach; tori is on top and to the side. Tori grabs uke's inside lapel (as close to the neck as possible) and forcefully brings the lapel under uke's chin. With the help of his other hand and torso, he does not let uke maneuver freely and starts moving (running ahead) toward uke's head, pulling the lapel that he has in his hand. Tori's shifting makes it impossible for uke to weaken the pressure on his neck and uke is forced to give in.

Figure 50. Choke technique running opposite lapel

Tomoe-Jime

Judo competition rules allow standing choke techniques. Usually the completion of the choke ends on the ground. Let's look at three variations of an attack in a standing position that end with the choking of the opponent.

Forearm Choke Technique "The Scissors"

Tori grabs a lapel on uke's jacket. The same hand is on top (thumb is under the jacket), and the opposite hand is below (thumb is on outside of jacket). The hands must be touching. The grab takes place near the collarbone.

Jerking both hands down, tori forces uke to bend over. Right as uke bends his head over, tori raises his outside hand and, without loosening his grip, puts his forearm on the back of uke's head.

Tori crosses his forearms, spreading his elbows apart. In order to increase the pressure and distract uke's attention, tori may drop to the floor, for example, falling on his side toward the same hand. (See Figure 51.)

Choke Technique "The Whirligig"

Tori grabs uke's opposite lapel at the collarbone level.

Without loosening his grip, he takes a half-step back, increasing the distance between them. Curving his back, he makes a complete turn around the longitudinal axis. At the same time, the lapels of uke's jacket start to tighten on uke's neck.

To increase the pressure and distract uke's attention, tori can move to the ground position.

The technique is completed by squeezing uke's neck with the hands.

Another variation of this technique differs in the initial grab. Tori grabs the outside lapel of uke's jacket. The turn is executed in the direction of the lower hand.

If the grab is above the collarbone, one turn is enough to ensure victory. If you are able to grab at the collarbone level or lower, you must continue to twist after one turn in order to tighten uke's jacket around his neck.

Forearm Counterchoke

With one hand, tori grabs the outside lapel of uke's jacket above the collarbone and with the second hand grabs the collar from inside (thumb is on

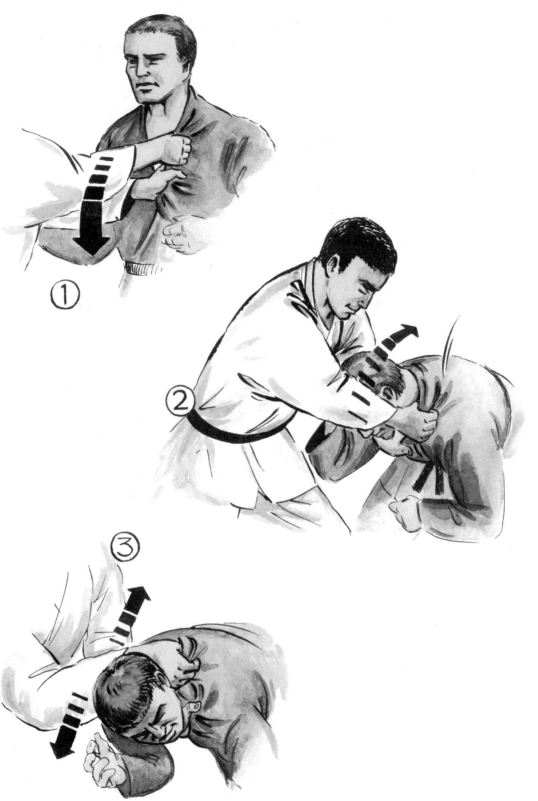

Figure 51 Choke technique with forearms, the scissors

Figure 52 Choke technique
the whirligig

the outside of the jacket). Turning his side to uke in the direction of the seized lapel, tori brings his forearms as close to each other as possible (exerting pressure on uke's neck).

In order to increase pressure and distract uke's attention, tori can move to a ground position: He falls on his back, turns around, and comes out on top.

Figure 53. Forearm counterchoke

JUDO

All three of the above variations of the standing choke techniques, even if the outcome is unsuccessful (uke doesn't lose consciousness or give in), ensure ideal conditions for continuing the attack on the ground by hold-downs.

Self-Defense Techniques

The main difference between judo and jujitsu is the absence in judo of striking techniques, without which fighting under conditions of a real-life threat to one's life and health is pointless. Nonetheless, in creating a new system of physical education, Jigoro Kano could not completely disregard judo's applied importance. The system of Kodokan would not be complete and applicable to real life without a set of self-defense techniques.

The classical set of self-defense techniques, kime-no-kata (another name is sinken-syobu-no-kata—a set of fighting techniques), is divided into two groups. The first group is done with partners kneeling down. This group has eight techniques. The second group is done standing and includes twelve techniques:

1. Breaking a two-arm hold
2. Breaking a sleeve hold from behind
3. Defending from a direct punch (to either the stomach or the head)
4. Defending from an uppercut
5. Defending from a blow to the head
6. Defending from a downward swinging blow
7. Defending from a groin kick
8. Defending from a two-arm torso grab from behind
9. Defending from a knife attack to stomach
10. Defending from an armed (knife, bottle) strike from above

11. Heading off an attempt to grab a sword from its scabbard (in the modern interpretation, heading off an attempt to reach for a pistol or revolver)

12. Defending from an overhead strike (with a long weapon, such as a stick, etc.)

The main criteria for the effectiveness of any system of hand-to-hand combat, which includes the combat section of judo, are simplicity and reliability. A minimum of various techniques, simple in the structure of their motions, that adequately resolve a given situation are required to allow you to develop an automatic skill that permits you to act effectively under conditions of a real-life threat. Using this as his starting point, Jigoro Kano used strikes as deflectors for setting up moves and a series of technical moves from the sport section of judo.

For example, the armlocking technique on the elbow from kime-no-kata is the "elbow lever" in the self-defense technique, hyperextension of the elbow joint beyond its natural range with a fixed wrist in the following variations:

1. Pressing down on the elbow with the palm

2. Pressing down with the chest

3. Pressing down on the elbow with the underarm

Choke techniques use the forearm or lapels from behind, and throws are based on major outer reaping (rear body drop), shoulder throw, and hip throw. For the uninitiated, this selection of technical moves, which may at first glance seem meaningless, is not very spectacular to watch, but in reality these moves are very reliable. It's no accident that, in slightly changed form, these techniques became the foundation of the well-tested practical combat system called sambo, which was used as a weapon by special services in the Soviet Union. These techniques came to the Soviet Union through Vasily Sergeevich Oshchepkov, who discovered the Kodokan when still a boy. Persistent lessons led to his becoming the first Russian to receive the judo master's black belt. Oshchepkov became one of the most colorful popularizers of judo, realizing the importance of this system of physical education and its applied methods for workers in law-enforcement agencies, intelligence, and security services.

Standing Self-Defense Techniques
Breaking a Frontal Two-Hand Grab

Tori grabs uke's wrists from above. Uke steps back, spreads his arms out, kicks tori in the groin; then, breaking free and grabbing tori's wrist, uke pulls his hand to his chest and, pressing down on the elbow with his armpit, executes an armlock.

Figure 54. Breaking a frontal two-hand grab

Breaking Free from a Rear Sleeve Grab

Tori grabs uke's opposite sleeve from behind.

Uke turns toward the seized hand, kicking tori's knee, and, continuing to turn, executes a major outer reaping.

Defending from a Direct Punch

Tori punches uke in the face with his right fist.

Variation 1

Uke, moving off the line of attack, grabs tori's arms, jerks him forward and down, steps behind his back, and executes a choke technique from behind with his forearm.

(See Figure 55.)

Figure 55. Defending from a direct punch
(variation 1)

Variation 2

Uke, leading with his left forearm, deflects tori's arm, grabs it, and, turning his back toward his opponent, executes a shoulder throw.

Figure 56. Defending from a direct punch
(variation 2)

Defending from an Uppercut to the Chin

Tori punches uke in the chin.

Uke leans back and away from the punch. He grabs tori's arm and, continuing the arm motion, lifts it upwards. Then, with a sharp turn, pulls the seized arm in to his chest and, bending over, executes an armlock on the elbow joint.

Figure 57. Defending from an uppercut to the chin

Defending from a Side Head Strike

Tori strikes uke's face from the side.

Uke, leaning away from the strike, blocks tori's arm with the opposite forearm and with his free hand strikes the opponent in the solar plexus. Ducking tori's arm, he grabs the opponent's back and free arm and executes a hip throw.

Figure 58. Defending from a side head strike

Defending from a Downward Swinging Strike

Tori takes a step with his left foot, raises his right hand as if to swing, and, stepping with his right leg, strikes downward and from the side.

Uke ducks away from the strike, steps behind tori's back, grabs the opposite lapel of tori's jacket, and executes a choke technique.

Figure 59. Defending from a downward swinging strike

Defending from a Direct Kick to Groin

Tori kicks with his right leg.

Uke steps off the line of attack, turning his left side to the opponent. He grabs tori's leg, jerks it forward, and lands a counterstrike on the opponent's support knee or in his groin.

Figure 60. Defending from a direct kick to groin

Breaking Free from a Two-Arm Rear Torso Grab

As the opponent is facing uke's back, he grabs uke's torso with his hands.

Uke, squatting slightly, spreads his arms out, weakening tori's grip. He grabs tori's arm and, standing on the same knee, executes a shoulder throw and strikes the prostrate opponent with his hand.

Figure 61. Breaking free from a two-arm rear torso grab

Defending from a Knife Attack to Abdomen

Tori attacks with a knife to the abdomen.

Uke, stepping off the line of attack, blocks the strike with the opposite forearm then grabs the armed hand with the same hand, steps behind the opponent's back, and, with his free hand, grabs the opposite lapel of his jacket. He executes an armlock technique on the elbow and, at the same time, a hold from behind with the lapel.

Figure 62. Defending from a knife attack to abdomen

Defending from an Overhead Weapon Attack

Tori strikes from above (with a bottle, club, etc.).

Uke blocks tori's hand with the opposite hand, grabs the arm with his other hand, and, pulling the opponent forward, squeezes the seized hand to his chest. Bending sharply, he executes an armlock on the elbow.

Figure 63. Defending from an overhead weapon attack

Self-Defense Developments by Mikonosuke Kawaishi

Another branch of judo's combat section is a system developed by Professor Mikonosuke Kawaishi. This man made an enormous contribution to the development of judo in Belgium and France, beginning his activities before the war. Kawaishi's sensei was Master Kurihara from the union of Butoku-Kai, which competed with the renowned Kodokan. Nonetheless, as far as the self-defense techniques of both schools go, they are basically those of jujitsu, making prodigious use of strike techniques.

In 1952 Kawaishi published his book *My Method of Self-Defense (Ma Methode de Self-Defense)*. The second part of the book is devoted entirely to *atemi*—techniques of finger strikes, strikes using the back of the hand, elbow, knee, foot strikes, and head butts. The significance of strikes in real-life combat is hard to overestimate. This technique can be used in the beginning phase of a counterattack to weaken and distract the opponent, in the main phase as a way of resolving a situation, and in the final phase to strike the finishing blow.

Whoever masters the basic throwing techniques of sport judo will not have any difficulty in studying combat judo. For purposes of self defense you can make active use of shoulder throws, hip throws, reapings, sweeps, and armlock techniques, which, following pain-inflicting diversionary strikes, are much easier to execute.

Below is a table showing the effectiveness of strikes of varying intensities on the human body's most sensitive areas. The numbers one through five indicate the degree of pain as a result of a blow landed with a certain amount of force on the indicated area:

1. First-degree pain. The pain is not strong but can throw your opponent into confusion and distract his attention.

2. Sharp pain. Throws your opponent into confusion for a greater amount of time.

3. The pain stuns your opponent and causes numbness in the tissue, despite the fact that your opponent is, as a rule, still conscious.

4. Temporary paralysis or loss of consciousness.

5. Serious injury, loss of consciousness, perhaps death.

Table 2. Pain zones on the human body and the impact of strikes in those areas

Strikes No.	Pain Zone		
	Light	Moderate	Hard
1. Temple	3	4	5
2. Eyes	3	4	5
3. Nose	2	3	4
4. Jaw	1	2	3
5. Chin	2	3	4
6. Side of Neck	2	3	4
7. Larynx	3	4	5
8. Shoulder	1	2	3
9. Collarbone	1	2	3
10. Armpit	1	2	3
11. Solar Plexus	2	3	4–5
12. Sub-costal Region	2	3	4
13. Groin Area	3	4	5
14. Biceps	1	2	3
15. Elbow	1	2	3
16. Forearm	1	2	3
17. Wrist	1	2	3
18. Back of Hand	1	2	3
19. Fingers	1	2	3
20. Thigh/Hip	1	2	3
21. Knee	2	3	4
22. Shin/Lower Leg	2	3	4
23. Ankle	1	2	3
24. Foot Arch	1	2	3
25. Base of Skull	3	4	5
26. Back of Neck	2	3	4
27. Seventh Neck Vertebra	3	4	5
28. Spinal Column, Chest Section	2	3	4

No.	Strikes	Pain Zone		
		Light	Moderate	Hard
29.	Coccyx	3	4	5
30.	Kidney Area	2	3	4
31.	Popliteal Cavity	1	2	3
32.	Calf Muscle	1	2	3
33.	Achilles Tendon	1	2	3

Professor Kawaishi's biography contains some interesting facts. After eleven years in Europe, he, along with his students, organized the French Judo and Jujitsu Federation in the spring of 1946. Then he returned to his homeland in order to get married. After that he set off for the Soviet Union and East Germany, where he spent around two years and apparently was in contact with local special services. In 1958, the renowned East German expert Horst Wolf published his book *Judo—Self-Defense (Judo—Selbstverteidigung)*, where he reproduces techniques suggested by Mikonosue Kawaishi. Perhaps the agents of one of the most professional organizations of its time, the Stasi, used these techniques in their special training. The same techniques of hand-to-hand combat are used in the special physical training of the agents of former Soviet and Russian law-enforcement agencies.

The School of Combat Sambo

For a long time the world has been familiar with the techniques of sport sambo, the Russian fighting style. National sambo federations have been created in dozens of countries, and numerous international competitions are held, including continental and world championships. Sport sambo is practiced by women as well.

As for combat sambo, the curtain of secrecy has only recently started to lift from this previously strictly confidential weapon. Combat sambo is an invisible weapon, but constantly in the possession of the one who has mastered it. This dangerous technique, whose chief criteria are simplicity and reliability, was refined for many years. The techniques of combat sambo are applicable both on the street and in the forest, day and night, winter and summer. There are no eye-catching leaps and fanciful poses, flowing body displacements, or rituals. On the outside it presents a rather unattractive, but most effective, spectacle.

It should be acknowledged that, besides the Kodokan graduate Vasily Sergeevich Oshchepkov, one unique man stands at the source of combat sambo. His name is Victor Afanasievich Spiridonov. Spiridonov was an officer of the Rusian army who fought in the Russo-Japanese War in Manchuria and a top expert in applied military gymnastics, a strong and nimble man who quickly appreciated jujitsu's merits.

After the Russian Revolution in 1917, Spiridonov took an active part in the creation of a system of combat training for employees of domestic affairs organizations. In 1922, Felix Dzerzhinsky, head of the state security service (known as the Cheka; its agents were called "chekists"), put before the Cheka the task of constantly perfecting their shooting and physical training. These qualities would not only ensure them success in their operations, but even to a certain degree safeguarded the chekists' lives in dangerous situations. The quickly formed athletic society Dynamo united athletes from the Cheka, border guards, and police officers. The Dynamo section soon became the Soviet Union center for the development of self-defense technique, strategy, and teaching methodology. It fell to Victor Spiridonov to begin this activity and direct its future course. The techniques he developed became the foundation for combat sambo.

Steps in Combat Sambo

In combat sambo, regardless of the nature and substance of an attack, there is a single algorithm of actions used in warding off an onslaught. This algorithm is the order of steps, each of which represents the resolution of a specific tactical objective:

Step 1: Minimize losses from your opponent's attack.

Step 2: Seize the initiative through diversionary actions.

Step 3: Get your opponent on his back.

Step 4: Execute a final, pain-causing action.

Depending on the situation, additional steps may be taken:

Step 5: Disarm your opponent.

Step 6: Search your opponent.

Step 7: Escort your opponent away.

Details of the Steps

Step 1

Objective: to minimize potential losses from a successful attack by your opponent.

If an opponent strikes (punching, kicking, or with a weapon), forceful blocks and props won't guarantee uke's safety. The most effective resolution is to step off the line of attack and, at the same time, deflect the attacking limb in the opposite direction.

There are two variations for stepping off the line of attack:

Variation 1: Your opponent punches (or kicks) you. Stepping forward and to the side with your opposite leg, deflect the attack toward your opponent, using your forearm or palm and turning parallel to the line of attack. In this variation, the limb used for attack ends up between the opponents.

Variation 2: Your opponent punches (or kicks) you. Stepping forward and to the side with the same leg, turn parallel to the line of attack, leaving your other leg back while deflecting the attacking limb away from your body. In this variation, the opponents end up tight against one another.

Step 2

Objective: to seize the initiative through pain-inflicting diversionary tactics.

After stepping off the line of attack, if you are able to avoid a serious initial defeat and maintain combat readiness, you need to launch a counterstrike, preferably an injury-causing action (armlock).

The nature and form of the diversionary action depend on the opponents' positioning to one another, their respective height and weight, type of clothing, etc.

In terms of convenience for launching a counterstrike, the preferred one is the second variation of the move off the line of attack, when your opponent remains completely open to a strike. In this position you should use the following strikes:

- Punch with free hand (other hand controls the attacking limb) to the face, chest, solar plexus, groin
- Finger poke to eyes
- Heel of palm to chin, nose, eyebrows
- Open-palm strike to cheek, ear
- Side elbow to jaw, temple, uppercut to chin
- Head butt to face, stomach
- Kick to groin, stomach, head (with various parts of the foot)
- Knee to groin, chest, stomach
- Kick with sole of foot to shin, knee
- Heel strike to arch of foot, toes

When the attacking limb is between opponents (the first variation of the move off the line of attack), it is more difficult to launch a diversionary attack. Nonetheless, there are several effective methods. These include the following:

- Back of fist with free hand to temple, forehead, nose
- Elbow to ribs, temple, jaw
- Head butt to face
- Kick to groin, knee, shin, arch of foot
- Knee to groin, chest, solar plexus

Step 3

Objective: to lay your opponent out on his back. If your opponent punches you, after moving off the line of attack according to variation 1, the following may be used to continue the attack:

Hand Squeeze. Grab your opponent's attack hand. Using your thumb pads, press into the middle of the back of your opponent's hand.

Turn the seized hand palm up, bring it down as low as possible, and, pressing down with your thumbs away from your body, force your opponent to fall on his back from the severe pain in his wrist.

Figure 64. Hand squeeze

Major Outer Drop. Using the leg furthest from your opponent, step behind the line of his heels. Squatting down on the far leg, place the near one between his legs. Using the bend in the elbow of the near arm, grab him by the neck, and, not allowing the opponent's near leg to step back and bending forward sharply, turn him on his back.

Figure 65. Major outer drop

Inside Straight Arm. Grabbing the wrist of the attack hand with the same hand, turn the palm away from your body and press down with the opposite armpit on your opponent's shoulder. Sharply bending forward, press your chest on his elbow, hyperextending his arm beyond its normal range. Using an armlock, throw your opponent face down.

Figure 66. Inside straight arm

Hair Grab Throw Down. Grabbing tori's wrist with the same hand, grab the hair on your opponent's head and, jerking him back toward his heels, throw him on his back.

Complications are possible in this maneuver. If you can't grab his hair (because it is too short, he is bald, or he is wearing some sort of head garb), you must grab his face at the same time that you strike his face (thumb turned down) with your palm (the one closest to your opponent's hand) and, with a downward motion away from your body, throw him on his back.

Figure 67. Hair grab throw down

Throw Down by Grabbing Clothing on Shoulders. Continuing the motion forward after stepping off the line of attack, turn your chest to the opponent's back, grab his clothing on the shoulders, and, moving back, throw the opponent on his back.

Complications are possible in this maneuver. If you can't grab the opponent's clothing, you must grab either his hair, with both hands, or his face. Pressing down on the eye sockets, continue your backward motion, throwing the opponent on his back.

(See Figure 68.)

Throat Grab Throw Down. Place the hand closest to the opponent on the back of his head and attack his throat with the other hand, squeezing the

Figure 68. Throw down by grabbing clothing on shoulders

cartilage of his larynx with your fingers. Throw the opponent's head back, squeezing the throat with a countermotion of the hands, and throw him on his back.

Throwing the opponent to the ground while stepping off the line of attack as described in variation 2 (when opponents are practically touching each other) can be accomplished in the following ways:

Figure 69. Throat grab throw down

Shoulder Throw. Grab your opponent's attack hand with the same hand near the elbow or a little higher. Jerk your opponent forward off balance, forcing him to rise up on the balls of his feet. Bend your knee slightly and, squatting down, turn your back to him. Grab your opponent's attack hand with your other hand and, pressing your back tightly against his chest, straightening your legs at the knees, and bending forward sharply, throw your opponent over your back.

Hip Throw. Grab your opponent's attack hand with your same hand near the elbow or a little higher. Pull your opponent off balance, forcing him to rise up on the balls of his feet. Turn your side toward him and, bending slightly at the knee and squatting down, wrap your free arm around your opponent's back from under his arm. Straightening your legs at the knee and shoving your opponent's pelvis with your hips while using your arms and turning your torso toward the seized hand, throw him on his back.

Major Outer Drop. Stepping away from your opponent with your far leg off the line of his heels, grab your opponent's neck with the elbow that is closer to him. Blocking your opponent's backward motion with the leg nearest to him and bending sharply forward, throw your opponent on his back.

Figure 70. Major outer drop

Face Shove Throw Down. Controlling your opponent's attack hand with the opposite hand while striking him near the nose with the palm of your free hand, shove your opponent's head down and away from your body and throw him on his back.

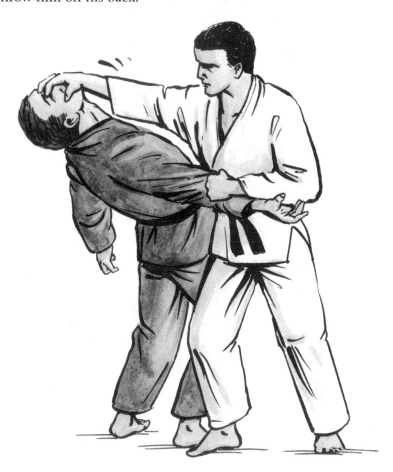

Figure 71. Face shove throw down

Head Grab Throw Down. Grab the top of your opponent's head with your near hand and his chin with the other hand. The fingers on both hands are directed away from your body. With a twisting motion, turn your opponent's head away while throwing him on his back.

Figure 72. Head grab throw down

Hair Grab Throw Down. Controlling your opponent's attack hand with your opposite hand, grab the hair on the back of your opponent's head and, continuing the motion in the direction of his free hand, throw him on his back with a jerk.

Complications may arise in this maneuver. If you can't grab his hair, you must strike your opponent's face with your palm and, pulling his head back, throw him to the ground.

(See Figure 73.)

Figure 73. Hair grab throw down

Step 4

Objective: to execute a final, injury-causing move, completely depriving your opponent of the ability to fight.

Final injury-causing actions (the final blow) must be executed primarily by the legs (heel, toes, knee) and with the arms only in exceptional circumstances. This is because, when a person falls on his back, inertia causes his legs to continue their forward movement upward. If, while this is happening, the person under attack maintains consciousness, he will single-mindedly try to kick tori's head. An especially dangerous strike is one aimed at the temple region; the likelihood that such a strike will hit its mark increases sharply as tori bends over in an attempt to punch the prostrate opponent.

We recommend preparing the final blow before the opponent starts falling, since only when someone is without any support—during the fall— is he unable to offer any active resistance. The feeling of support, especially when prostrate on the ground, serves as a signal for continuing active countermoves.

Depending on the distance and position of your prostrate opponent, strikes are executed on the following areas (see table 3):

Table 3.

Distance	Positioned to side of opponent	
Far	Toe	Ribs
Near	Heel	Ribs, Sternum
Up close	Knee	Ribs, Sternum
	Positioned above head	
Far	Toe	Temple, Top of Head
Near	Heel	Temple, Forehead
Up close	Knee	Collarbone, Sternum

A heel strike is delivered from above downward in a vertical line.

A toe strike is similar to a soccer kick.

Tori can use his knee to inflict injury by bringing it down sharply with all his weight on the opponent's rib cage.

If after the opponent falls tori remains positioned near the prostrate opponent's legs, the final blow is delivered by a knee to the groin.

Step 5

Objective: to disarm the opponent.

Disarming a knife-wielding opponent is done after throwing him to the ground and executing a traumatizing action by:

- Striking the back of the armed hand (with the heel, base of fist, base of palm)
- Pressing down with the base of the palm on the smooth plane of the blade in the direction of the pinky finger of the armed hand (or in the direction of the thumb, depending on how the weapon was grabbed)
- Squeezing the hand, stabilizing the elbow of the armed hand

Back at the turn of the century, the expressions "leadership for police officials" and "self-defense and arrest" underscored the idea that, by starting a given technique, you must remember that the health of a human being is more valuable than anything, and, therefore, techniques that cause severe pain should be resorted to only when you are faced with a dangerous criminal and when your life is in danger. Armed actions are always either fatal or dangerous for the life and health of the one they are directed against. Most important is to avoid bloodshed; however decisive the self-defense technique may be, it is less dangerous for the life of a person who is occasionally drunk, insane, or unfortunate than an action involving the use of weapons.

Furthermore, knowing self-defense techniques and being able to apply them in a variety of situations is very useful, **but the most important thing is to learn how to conduct oneself safely in society so that it won't be necessary to use the techniques.**

Foundation Techniques of Combat Sambo: Disarming Techniques

Opponent Attacks with Knife from Above (Knife Is in Right Hand)

Variation 1. Armlock Technique "Inside Straight Arm"

1. Block your opponent's armed hand with your right forearm, at the same time moving off the line of attack by stepping forward with your right leg and turning your body away from your opponent.

2. With your right hand, grab your opponent's right hand near the wrist and, at the same time, kick him in the groin (with your shin).

3. Setting your right leg back and to the right, pull the seized hand toward your body and execute an armlock at the elbow, pressing your chest down on the elbow beyond its natural extension.

4. Force your opponent to discard the knife because of the severe pain.

(See Figure 74.)

Figure 74. Armlock technique inside straight arm

Variation 2. Armlock "Upper Arm Knot"

1. Using your left forearm, block your opponent's armed hand while stepping off the line of attack by stepping forward with your left leg and turning your body away from your opponent.

2. Grab the forearm of the armed hand with your left hand and with your right hand grab the elbow of the armed hand from below while kicking the groin (with your shin).

3. With a sharp movement of the arms, pull the elbow of the seized arm in toward your body and, at the same time, shove the forearm of the seized hand away from your body with your left hand.

4. Step behind your opponent with your right leg and execute a major outer drop.

5. By twisting the elbow and shoulder joints of the armed hand, force your opponent to discard his weapon.

Figure 75. Armlock arm knot from above

Opponent Attacks with Knife from Below (Knife in Right Hand)

Variation 1. Armlock "Arm Bend Behind Back"

1. Step forward with your left leg while blocking the armed hand with your left forearm.

2. Step off the line of attack, turning your torso away from your opponent.

3. Grab the elbow of your opponent's armed hand with your right arm while kicking him in the groin (with your shin).

4. Turning your torso to the left, pull him in by his elbow with your right hand and shove him away from your body with your left hand. Bend the arm at the elbow, and force your opponent to transfer his center of gravity to his right leg.

5. Stepping back with your right leg, put the forearm of the seized arm in your left hand.

6. With your right arm grab his hair (or face).

7. Execute an armlock on the elbow of the armed hand, raising your left elbow upward and pulling your opponent's head toward your body.

8. Force your opponent to discard his weapon and cease resistance.

(See Figure 76.)

Variation 2. Armlock "Hand Squeeze"

1. Step forward with left foot while blocking the armed hand with your left forearm.

2. Step off the line of attack, turning your torso away from your opponent.

3. Grab the wrist of the armed hand with your left hand.

4. Strike the armed hand with your right hand, dislodging the knife. If you are unable to dislodge the knife, kick your opponent in the groin, grab the armed hand with both hands so that your thumbs are on the back of the hand, and bend the seized hand toward the forearm; turn your torso to the left and, twisting the seized hand outward and stepping to the left, throw your opponent over and kick him in the head or torso, making it impossible for him to fight.

(See Figure 77.)

Figure 76. Armlock hand behind back

Figure 77. Armlock
"Hand Squeeze"

Theoretical Training

In one-on-one competitive matches, special importance should be given to theoretical training. Pedagogical observations made over the years and the analysis of competitive activity of judoka of various classifications make it clear that the level of theoretical and, as a result, tactical preparedness of judoka lag behind their physical and technical preparedness. The inability to come up with a preliminary plan of attack in a match against an opponent known to you in advance, the lack of developed abilities to act in standard situations, and the fear that unexpected situations will emerge or be created in a match all have a fatal effect on performance and hamper the growth of skill.

Compared to other forms of fighting, judo stands apart for its great arsenal of allowable technical actions. This, in turn, assumes an endless variety of situations that can arise during the course of a match. Nonetheless, one can divide this variety up into a series of standard situations that are encountered in competitive matches. These situations can be offered as models that facilitate the development of tactical thinking and an ability to act rationally in quickly changing circumstances.

Success in resolving a task in any sphere of human activity depends on the difficulty of the task. The very same task can be made easier if ways of resolving it are known or if it has been resolved before. If a difficult task is repeatedly resolved and one learns to resolve it automatically, the task becomes much simpler. This also applies to the motor tasks characteristic of judo.

The use of problem model situations in lessons and training is prudent from a methodological point of view. The resolution of a model situation occurs under prearranged conditions. As a game, this makes the training process more varied, enlivens it, and increases the effectiveness of lessons. The objective of a lesson is built on the following principle: to teach judoka to relate special theoretical knowledge and motor skills to the demands of competition.

Possessing a range of knowledge, abilities, and skills, and experience in using technical and tactical actions in a competitive situation, is an essential condition for learning to resolve situations correctly. With this goal, we have worked out a list of possible variations for the development of an attack. There are four phases of an attack:

1. Fighting for a convenient attack grab. This phase of the attack can unfold under various conditions:

   a) Opponent in right-hand stance.

   b) Opponent in left-hand stance.

   c) Opponent evades grab through maneuvering.

   d) Opponent breaks grab.

   e) Opponent executes blocking grabs.

   f) Opponent ducks under arms away from grab, attempting to counterattack, etc.

2. Preparing the throw. Throws can be executed in the following situations:

   a) Opponent moves forward.

   b) Opponent moves back.

   c) Opponent moves left.

   d) Opponent moves right.

In addition:

   a) Opponent may be in low stance.

   b) Opponent may be in high stance.

   c) Opponent may try to attack with a given grab.

   d) This phase of the attack can unfold in the "red zone."

3. Executing the throw. The throw can once again be executed in various circumstances:

   a) Opponent offers vigorous and powerful resistance.

b) Opponent sinks down abruptly.

c) Opponent maneuvers away.

d) Opponent executes standing counterattack.

4. Transition to ground fighting. This can be done under various conditions as well:

a) Uke is on his stomach; tori is on top.

b) Uke is on his back; tori is on top.

c) Uke is on his back; tori is on top astride.

d) Uke is on his back with tori on top between uke's legs.

e) Uke is on his stomach with tori kneeling in front of him above his head.

One way to increase a judoka's theoretical preparedness may be by including special lessons in the training process. These lessons include the following:

■ Detailed sorting of variations of actions in the situations described above

■ Written plans of action by judoka in specific situations

Special knowledge ensures a precondition for mastering higher skills when an objective analysis of a given situation under time constraints allows judoka to produce a motor skill that ensures the maximum result.

Objective Evaluation of Skill Level in Judo

Obtaining information about a judoka's technical arsenal, fighting style, and the strong and weak points in his competitive preparedness is provided by a stenographic record of competitive activity. All of a judoka's actions in a match are recorded in a special protocol by a system of symbols, which reflect which techniques the judoka used, what grades and notations he received, and what actions his opponent used; the time parameters of the match are also recorded. Deciphering the record, processing the data, and the corresponding analysis allow for an objective assessment of a judoka's technical and tactical level of preparedness.

It is customary to use the following symbols in the stenographic recording:

Table 4.

Name of Technique	Symbol
Body Drop	∠
Major Outer Drop	╱
Inner Thigh Throw	⋏
Two-Leg Throw	A
Major Inner Reaping	2
Minor Outside Reap	Ƅ
Minor Inner Hook	2x
Hip Throw	⌽
Back Shoulder-Grab Throw	⌽
Back Underarm-Grab Throw	⌽
One-Arm Shoulder Throw	↙изн
One-Arm Under-the-Shoulder Throw	↙пт
Inner Wheel	↙б
Ankle Sweep	↙к
Advancing Foot Sweep	Bр
Knee Wheel	Bт
Floating Drop	T
Corner Drop	Tz
Circle Throw	↑x
Corner Reversal	⇑
Shoulder Wheel "The Mill"	↑
Two-Leg Throw	↑
Ankle-Grab Throw	↟
Hip-Grab Throw	Я
Shin-Grab Throw	↑п
Back Throw	↑б

Name of Technique	Symbol
Scoop Throw	У
Side Scoop Throw	У
Holds	Ⴒ
Armlocks	
Choke Techniques	

Table 5.

Grades		Instructions	
Ippon	(■)	Shido	(sh)
Waza-Ari	(wA)	Chui	(ch)
Yuko	(Y)	Kei-koku	(kk)
Koka	(K)	Hansoku-Make	(H/m)

Grading Competitive Activity

A judoka's competition grade is based on an analysis of technical and tactical indicators that characterize the athlete's level of readiness.

1. The technical and tactical indicator "Activity" indirectly characterizes the motor and functional readiness of a judoka and is expressed in the number of attack actions executed by him or her in one minute:

$$A = \frac{N}{t} \text{ (атак в минуту)},$$

where N = $n + n1$

                N = general number of fighter's attack actions

                n = number of graded attack actions

              $n1$ = number of actual attacks by judoka

                t = time of fight

The activity can be graded in an analysis of one match, a match conducted within the framework of a single competition, or in an analysis of matches in a series of competitions.

For example, in the course of a match, a judoka executes four successful attacks (n) and actually attacked (n1) six times. The match lasted 5 minutes (t).

So the fighter's activity in this match is:

$$A = \frac{4+6}{5} = \frac{10}{5} = 2$$

This means that the judoka attempts an attack every 30 seconds in the course of a match. This is a rather good indicator that corresponds to the rules of competition that require the judoka to conduct an active, offensive fight.

If it is necessary to analyze the judoka's activity during the course of an entire tournament, then all his attacks (graded and ungraded) should be summarized and the general length of fighting time determined.

For example, the judoka had five meetings, two of which ended before the clock ran out. The general fighting time was 18 minutes 15 seconds. The number of points was twelve, and the number of actual attacks was twenty-eight.

Then   Тогда $A = \dfrac{12 + 28}{18.25} = \dfrac{40}{18.25} = 2.2$

The model "Activity" indicator in a match is three. That is, the judoka should attack every 20 seconds.

2. The technical-tactical indicator "Reliability of Attack Actions," which characterizes the effectiveness of a judoka's attacks, is determined according to the following formula:

$$Ha = \frac{n}{N} \times 100 \ (\%).$$

Let's use the same values as in the previous example. The reliability of the attack actions in one match:

$$Ha = \frac{4}{4+6} \times 100\% = \frac{4}{10} \times 100\% = 0.4 \times 100\% = 40\%.$$

This means that the judoka earns a grade in four out of ten attacks.

The reliability of the attack actions over the course of an entire tournament is:

$$Ha = \frac{12}{12+28} \times 100\% = \frac{12}{40} \times 100\% = 0.3 \times 100\% = 30\%.$$

This value for the indicator suggests that three out of ten attacks were successful.

A "Reliability of Attack Actions" indicator of 50 percent may serve as the model value in a match (five out of ten of the judoka's attacks must be evaluated), that is, every other attack should be successful.

3. The technical-tactical indicator "Successfulness" determines the quality of the judoka's attack actions. Put another way, this is the average grade of the judoka's attack actions.

Despite the fact that grades in judo aren't totaled (the quality of the mark is considered the most important thing), it is generally held that a clean victory, or Ippon, corresponds to ten conventional units, the grade Waza-Ari corresponds to seven, the grade Yuko to five, and the grade Koka to three. By knowing the number of grades earned by the judoka and their quality, you can calculate their average value or "Successfulness."

$$P = \frac{10 \times I + 7 \times WA + 5 \times Y + 3 \times K}{n}$$

I = number of Ippon grades; WA = number of Waza-Ari; Y = number of Yuko; and K = the number of Koka.

For example, twelve graded actions by someone in a competition were comprised of two Ippon, three Waza-Ari, five Yuko, and two Koka. Plugging these values into the formula, we get the following:

$$P = \frac{10 \times 2 + 7 \times 3 + 5 \times 5 + 3 \times 2}{12} = \frac{72}{12} = 6.0.$$

Thus, the average mark of this judoka's attack actions is "greater than Yuko."

It is recommended that you calculate the technical-tactical indicators "Successfulness in Standing Position" and "Successfulness in Ground Fighting" separately.

To achieve high performance levels in judo one should strive for an average score for standing attack actions of around seven (Waza-Ari). "Successfulness in Ground Fighting" should aim for Ippon.

4. The technical-tactical indicator "Defense Reliability" characterizes the judoka's ability to withstand an opponent's attack moves.

It is determined by the formula:

$$H_3 = \frac{N_{np} - n_{np}}{n_{np}} \times 100\%,$$

where n_{np} = the number of grades lost by the judoka, and N_{np} = the total number of attack actions by the opponent (opponents).

Thus $(N_{np} - n_{np})$ is the number of deflected attacks. A "Defense Reliability" indicator equal to 100 percent may be considered the model value.

5. The technical-tactical indicator "Combination Factor" characterizes the judoka's ability to use difficult technical and tactical moves in achieving victory in a match, not interrupting an attack that has been initiated, and continuing in an organic fashion a ground fighting attack that began in a standing position.

The quantitative value of the indicator is determined according to the formula:

$$K = \frac{k}{N} \times 100 \, (\%).$$

For example, in five meetings, out of forty graded and ungraded attack actions (N) the judoka conducted sixteen in combinations (transition from one technique to another) and in clusters (continuing an attack with a ground attack follow-up) (k). So, plugging the values into the formula, we get:

$$K = \frac{16}{40} \times 100\% = 0.4 \times 100\% = 40\%.$$

This means that four out of ten attacks were conducted by the judoka in combinations and in clusters. A "Combination Factor" in excess of 50 percent may be considered the model indicator. That is, complex technical and tactical actions must be used in every other attack.

6. The technical and tactical indicator "Variation" characterizes the variety of technique in a judoka's arsenal. The indicator is determined by the number of classification groups whose technical and tactical actions the judoka tried to conduct—"General Variation" (Vg)—and the number of classification groups whose technical and tactical moves were rated as "Effective Variation" (Ve).

For example, forty attacks (graded and ungraded) were comprised of body drops, major outer drop, inner thigh throw, major inner reaping and minor outer reaping, leg throws, front wheels, holds, choke techniques, and armlocks.

The "General Variation" of the judoka's technique would then be comprised of a five in standing position (number of techniques from different classification groups: drops, wheels, reapings, throws, and leg throws), and a three in ground fighting (holds, choke techniques, and armlocks).

Grades were received for body drops, inner thigh throw, minor outer reaping, and holds. So the "Effective Variation" of the judoka's technique from a standing position is three (number of techniques from different classification groups), and in ground fighting it is one.

The greater the variety of technique demonstrated by the judoka the more chances he has of building various tactical variations in a match.

Health

Staying in Your Weight Category or Switching to Another One

Currently judo competitions are held in the following weight categories: for men, under 60 kg/132 lbs., under 66 kg/145 lbs., under 73 kg/161 lbs., under 81 kg/179 lbs., under 90 kg/198 lbs., under 100 kg/220 lbs., and over 100 kg/220 lbs. For women the weight categories are under 48 kg/106 lbs., under 52 kg/115 lbs., under 57 kg/126 lbs., under 63 kg/139 lbs., under 70 kg/154 lbs., under 78 kg/172 lbs., and over 78 kg/172 lbs. In addition, tournaments have the Open category, where, theoretically, participants of any weight class can fight.

There are two methods for artificially regulating body mass, or, simply put, losing weight. The first is short-term (one to two days) or forced. The other—dispersed—can last from one to four weeks.

In addition, we can recommend the following variations for these methods:

1. "Even": The judoka, over the whole period of weight control, sheds approximately the same amount of weight (1 lb., 1.5 lbs., 2 lbs., etc.) on a daily basis.

2. "Shock": In the first two days the judoka sheds up to 50 percent of excess weight. Thereafter the daily percentage of lost weight gradually decreases.

3. "Gradually increasing": The amount of weight loss increases by the last day of the diet.

4. "Shock intervals": Over the course of two to four days, the judoka forcibly sheds 2 to 6 lbs. Then that weight is maintained for several days, and the cycle is repeated.

5. "Vacillating": Over an extended period of time, weight loss is divided into short-term periods of small increases.

For losing up to 10 percent of body mass, the even and gradually increasing methods are used most often. If more, then the accelerated-dispersed, shock interval, and vacillating methods are used.

An intensive training regimen (cross-training, games), weight-loss suits, Russian steam bath, sauna, and diet are also used as weight-loss methods.

The accelerated weight loss diet places a significant burden on the judoka's body, which is shown by biochemical changes in blood vessels. If the body dehydrates during training sessions, these changes have a cumulative effect, and workout efficiency is considerably reduced. Under these conditions even a moderate workout can be excessive. As a consequence, the judoka will experience burnout, diminished performance, and illness.

Training loads in an accelerated regimen should be in inverse proportion to water depletion and mineral metabolism. At the same time, the number of competitions must also be curtailed.

Greater training loads and high intensity may be used when weight loss is gradual.

Rules for a Rational Judo Diet

Success in training and competition for any judoka depends in large part on diet. Large amounts of physical stress require adequate stores of energy. In addition, profuse sweating, potential injuries from falling, skin abrasions, and minor injuries, without which any system of fighting would be impossible, require special attention to diet so as to speed the healing and recuperation processes.

It is not enough to have an abundance of food; you must be armed with knowledge about the nutritional value of food, a proper dietary regimen, and hygienic conditions that ensure high-quality food products.

Sports nutrition is a rather well-developed area, and, based on the issues raised in this field, it is possible to make scientifically sound recommendations.

Proteins

Proteins are the basic component of any living organism. They are the building blocks of all cells, tissues, and organs. The constant growth processes of cells and tissues require proteins. It is no accident that they are called proteins, which in Greek means "the first" or "most important." Therefore, proteins are an absolutely essential and irreplaceable component of any diet. Proteins help in the formation of enzymes and hormones that are very important for the body's vital activity.

Proteins contain nitrogen, and when they decompose they form various amino acids. Proteins can't be assimilated by the body directly. In the process of digestion, proteins pass through a complicated path of breaking down into amino acids, which are absorbed into the blood and used by the body's cells in that form.

Proteins are divided into complete and incomplete, according to their amino acid composition. Complete proteins contain the essential amino acids (approximately twelve), which are indispensable for the body. These are mainly animal proteins and individual plant proteins. Protein deficiency has an especially marked effect on a young, growing body.

More than half of the proteins must be of animal origin. The most valuable ones for athletes are milk, meat, fish, eggs, and dairy proteins. The most valuable proteins in plant products are in certain grains—buckwheat, rice, oats—and in beans, especially in soy, as well as in vegetables and potatoes.

When food contains proteins that vary in their amino acid composition, it meets a requirement that humans have for them. A dish like buckwheat oatmeal with milk is an example of a successful combination of proteins. Amino acids that are not in buckwheat are supplemented by amino acids found in milk.

Athletes in sports that demand a quick concentration of significant exertions, abrupt movements, and quick reactions need to consume large quantities of protein. Judoka need 2.4 to 2.5 g of protein for every kilogram (2.2 lbs.) of weight per day.

Fats

Combined with proteins, fats form cell structure, serve as a source of heat energy, prevent excessive heat loss from the body, provide the body with several vitamins, are a supplemental source of water, protect the body from mechanical injuries, and maintain efficiency, which is especially important for athletes.

In the human body, animal fats are stored when there is too much of them in foods and when foods contain too many carbohydrates, since carbohydrates and proteins are partly used for building fats.

Many animal fats contain vitamins. Fats also play an important role in the body's assimilation of vitamins found in other food products. Fish fat is rich in vitamins. Plant fats, despite their high assimilability and calorie content, have no vitamins.

Research in recent years has demonstrated the especially important role of vegetable oils, which contain a series of acids that are essential for the body in terms of fat metabolism and normal functioning of the liver.

There are many vegetable oils in canned fish (sprats, sardines, cod), canned vegetables (vegetable marrow, eggplant), and mayonnaise. Milk and egg yolk fats, as well as tissue fats (liver, bone marrow), contain vitamins. Fats that are in milk are rather rich in vitamins (especially during the summer) and are assimilated easily by the body.

Athletes require 100 to 120 g of fat a day, of which 80 percent should be of animal origin. From this, 90 percent should come from dairy fats (solid and melted butter contain 84 to 95 percent fat; sour cream contains 23.5 percent fat; and cream contains 20 percent).

Milk and sour-milk products (kefir, yogurt, cottage cheese) should definitely be included in the judoka's daily intake.

Carbohydrates

Carbohydrates are the human body's basic source of energy. They are essential for muscle activity, maintaining body temperature, and carrying out various internal bodily processes. When they enter the body, they are subject to decomposition, forming sugar (glucose), which is quickly absorbed and transported with the blood to all of the body's organs and systems. When it enters cells, glucose provides them with essential energy. Excess sugar is stored mainly in the liver and muscles, as well as in all tissues and cells (except nerve cells). This store is released during periods of heightened activity. As compared with proteins and fats, carbohydrates decompose significantly faster and, when necessary, are quickly brought out of storage in the liver and muscles.

Products of plant origin are the main sources of carbohydrates: sugar, white bread, pasta, potatoes, grains, peas, beans, fruits, chocolate, raisins, honey, jelly, jam, etc. Carbohydrates generally comprise about two thirds of a person's diet. When 1 g breaks down, the body receives 4.1 major calories.

When training for competition, sugar and other easily absorbed carbohydrates have a great practical significance for athletes, since their potential energy can be converted quickly for use.

When carbohydrates entering the body are not fully used, part of them are stored as fat. When carbohydrates are deficient in one's diet, fat breaks down and compensates for this deficiency. Athletes require at least 600 g of carbohydrates per day. Of this, sugar (sugar, candy, preserves, jam, fruit) should make up about 35 percent, and the remaining 65 percent should come from bread, potatoes, pasta, peas, beans, etc.

The practice observed with many athletes of consuming large quantities of sugar on a daily basis is wholly unfounded. Sugar is not only a food product but also an irritant for the nervous system and a whole host of internal iron secretions. Large quantities of sugar cause a sharp increase of it in the blood. A one-time intake of more than 150 g of sugar exits the body in your urine. Repeated dosages of large quantities of sugar are possible only in special situations before the start of and after prolonged athletic activity.

The body stores carbohydrates in amounts of 300 to 400 g, but for athletes in peak training this number rises to 500 g. In periods of intense athletic activity, carbohydrates are released at the rate of around 150 g an hour. Thus, a 3 to 4 hour workout will exhaust the store of carbohydrates in the body; efficiency starts to quickly diminish and the athlete sometimes has a hard time finishing the workout or competition.

Vitamins

Vitamins strengthen one's resistance to disease-carrying microbes, improve efficiency, and facilitate the normal course of metabolic processes in the body. A vitamin deficiency in the diet leads to specific illnesses known under the general name of avitaminosis.

Vitamins A, the B group, C, D, P, K, PP, E, and other groups are important for the judoka.

Vitamin A (retinal, axerophthol) is considered a growth stimulator and is known as the beauty vitamin. It is the vitamin of resistance—without it the judoka exposes himself to risk of disease.

Vitamin A plays an essential role in normal vision. Vitamin A speeds healing and epitelization of the skin when it is damaged. This vitamin is found only in foods of animal origin: cream, egg yolk, liver, meat, cod, perch, etc. In the human body it is also formed from a substance known as carotene, a good source of which are carrots, red peppers, leeks, tomatoes, spinach, salad, sorrel, apricots, peaches, mandarins, and oranges. It is important to know that vitamin A is fat soluble; therefore, for greatest assimilation, you must make sure that it is in dishes with foods rich in this vitamin.

Vitamin E (tocopherol) is connected with metabolic processes in the muscles. The muscles are especially sensitive to vitamin E deficiency. Vitamin E is found in many foods, but only ones of vegetable origin and usually in small quantities (in grass buds, unrefined vegetable oils, egg yolk, and salad greens).

Vitamin E occurs in the largest levels in nettles, whose juice contains blood-forming properties. Then come corn, asparagus, and celery.

Vitamin D (calcipherol) regulates calcium and phosphorus deposits in the bones. Various rheumatic conditions (back pain and lumbago) can be a sign of a deficiency in this vitamin. Fish (salmon, mackerel, and lamprey) contains the highest levels of vitamin D.

The best foods in this regard are cod liver and herring. In addition, this is one of the vitamins that are formed in the human body when the skin is exposed to sunlight.

Vitamin K is a styptic vitamin, essential for blood clotting and for the production of protrombine. A lack of vitamin K in various parts of the body can lead to hemorrhaging, poor clotting, and anemia. Vitamin K is found in green leafy vegetables, in soy oil, kidney, casein (found in cheese), walnuts, cabbage, spinach, and tomatoes. It is found in large quantities in pine needles and in the leaves of the lucerne tree.

Vitamin C (ascorbic acid) is the most essential vitamin, which the human body requires constantly. Accumulation is almost impossible. An overabundance of vitamin C is not harmful, since any excess quantity is expelled from the body. Vitamin C increases iron assimilation, has antiscurvy properties, and flushes excess cholesterol out of the arteries.

With heightened muscle activity it facilitates increased endurance and speeds recuperation. It increases the body's capacity for resistance to infectious diseases, facilitates the fast healing of wounds, bone growth, and a normal pregnancy. Before, during, and after competitions the required amount of vitamin C increases to 250 to 300 mg a day. Working or training under conditions of extreme temperatures requires increased dosages of vitamin C.

Foods that are the most rich in vitamin C include vegetables, fruits, and berries. Black currants, dogrose, and green walnuts contain especially high levels of vitamin C. It occurs in high levels in oranges, lemons, Antonovka apples, wild strawberries, gooseberries, red tomatoes, cabbage, red peppers, horseradish, salad, and spinach.

The B Group of Vitamins

There are around thirty different kinds of B vitamins. They are all water soluble; all are included in the composition of enzymes; and all function very well even in small quantities. Almost all B-group vitamins can be found in yeast, liver, and bread grains.

Vitamin B$_1$ is essential for the central and peripheral nervous systems. The absence of vitamin B$_1$ causes weakened memory, fatigue, lack of self-confidence, shyness, nervousness, disruption of the digestive tract, pains in the extremities, in particular leg muscles, and shortness of breath. Clearly it would be impossible to train with such ailments. High performance in athletic contests would be out of the question.

They say that this vitamin creates optimists, since it does indeed eliminate fatigue, anxiety, and irascibility.

Vitamin B$_1$ is important for judo training, since it ensures better use of carbohydrates during muscle activity. The more carbohydrates are used up, the greater the demand for vitamin B$_1$.

Vitamin B$_1$ is found mostly in rye and wheat bread (made from coarse-grained flour), in bean plants—peas, haricot beans, lentils—and brewer's and baker's yeast, cabbage, carrots, potatoes, and meat, especially pork, brains, liver, etc.

The daily allowance of vitamin B_1 is 3 mg. When this vitamin is consumed in larger quantities than the body needs, it is quickly expelled and is not stored in the body. Vitamin B_1 content in foods does not fluctuate with the seasons.

Vitamin B_2 (riboflavin) participates in the restoration of organs and tissues and in the healing of wounds and ulcers. Vitamin B_2 deficiency shows up in diseases of the skin and mucous membranes.

Combined with vitamin A, vitamin B_2 facilitates sharpened vision. Vitamin B_2 is found in foods of both animal and plant origin. It is usually found with vitamin B_1. It is found in high levels in yeast and whole grains, as well as meat, liver, egg yolk, and milk; it is not found in many vegetables, just like vitamin B_1.

Vitamin B_3 (PP) prevents diseases of the skin, digestive organs, and the central nervous system and helps fight off cholesterol deposits and other fats in blood vessels and fights off "arthritic deposits" by soothing pain. Vitamin B_3, niacin, and nicotineamide are essential for the brain. Vitamin PP is found in wheat, buckwheat, mushrooms, brewer's and baker's yeast, peas and beans, meat (especially in turkey meat), liver, and kidneys.

Vitamin B_6 (pyridoxin) has a recommended daily allowance of around 2 mg a day. Young people require much more, as do those who are trying to lose weight.

Good sources of pyridoxin are walnuts, hazelnuts, and buckwheat oatmeal. B_6 is found in yeast, liver, pork, haricot beans, cabbage, and carrots.

Vitamin B_{12} (cyanocobalamine) deficiency will bring on anemia. The recommended daily allowance is around 3 mcg. If you eat meat and eggs and drink milk, you are getting an average of around 15 mcg a day. Aside from yeast, vitamin B_{12} is found only in foods of animal origin, primarily liver, fish, and seafood. Herring is exceptionally rich in B_6 and B_{12}.

Other B-group Vitamins

Vitamin H (biotine) is necessary in the body's ability to fight diseases, and for fortifying the skin, nails, and hair. Aside from yeast and liver, biotine can be found in chocolate, red cabbage, mushrooms, and peas.

There is a whole group of substances called **vitamin P.** This is rutin, citrine, and bioflavonoides. Their main role is to facilitate vitamin C assimilation.

An important function is in fortifying the capillaries. Subcutaneous hemorrhaging from small vessels damaged as a result of traumatic events (which often happens in judo) causes hematomes. For quick healing vitamin P is essential.

The richest sources of vitamin P are rowanberry fruits. Many of these compounds are in the fruit of the sea buckthorn, dogrose, black currants, and grapes, as well as green parsley, salad, capsicum, and buckwheat.

Minerals

Calcium, phosphorus, potassium, sodium, magnesium, iron, sulfur, chlorine, and other mineral elements are an important component of food. They make up the body's tissue cells. Their role in diet is great, despite the fact that they do not provide energy and their daily requirement is only 20 to 30 g. Studies have shown that minerals are important in minute amounts (microelements): copper, manganese, zinc, cobalt, lithium, iodine, fluorine, chrome, uranium, and many others. They take part in all complex biochemical processes that occur in the human body.

Mineral substances are also essential for the formation of blood, digestive juices, etc. They ensure the preservation of tissue protein properties and also strengthen or weaken the effect of enzymes.

Minerals are expelled mainly in the urine, sweat, etc. In the course of a 24-hour period, a relatively constant amount of minerals is being expelled from the body. They increase sharply only under conditions of increased perspiration, which happens frequently in training. Therefore, the body's mineral requirements depend on the degree to which they are expelled from the body. All essential elements for the human body are found in various foods, with the exception of cooking salt, which must be added to food in its pure form.

Under conditions of active training, phosphorous, calcium, potassium, and sodium are depleted in large quantities. This depletion must be compensated for. Judoka should know that various phosphate compounds found in the muscles play an exceptional role in muscle atrophy, especially when muscles are working at maximum intensity. Phosphate compounds influence reaction speed and muscle activity requiring high nerve tension. Phosphorous, calcium, and magnesium strengthen the skeleton.

Phosphorous occurs at high levels in meat and meat products, fish (cod, sturgeon, and herring), roe, milk, cottage cheese, cheeses, carrots, onions, buckwheat, oats, wheat, peas, haricot beans, lentils, and soy. Canned goods, haricot beans, dairy products (milk, cottage cheese, and cheese) fish roe, and lentils are rich in calcium. Iron is found in blood brawns and sausages, liver, and strawberries. Magnesium is found in large quantities in cheese, oats, and bean sprouts. Increasing the amount of calcium chloride in the diet improves assimilation of proteins and carbohydrates, and an increase in the amount of cooking salt facilitates better assimilation of fats. Assimilation of mineral salts, in turn, is higher under a carbohydrate regimen than under a protein one.

Mineral substances found in foods of animal origin are 90 to 98 percent assimilated, while those of vegetable origin are only 50 percent assimilated.

Calcium is essential for strengthening bone tissue. A deficiency in calcium and vitamin D can cause pain in the hip and chest areas of the spinal column. The most accessible and comparatively rich sources of calcium are milk and dairy products: cheese and cottage cheese. There is a lot of calcium in sprats, herring, green parsley, leafy cabbage, corn, horseradish, and garlic.

Zinc plays an important role in the growth and healthy state of the reproductive organs. It has a beneficial influence on the skin, nails, and hair. Zinc is found most abundantly in oysters (270 to 600 mg per kg), then bran, wheat sprouts (130 to 200 mg per kg), and most mushrooms (75 to 140 mg per kg). There is zinc in fish and liver, but in smaller quantities.

Iron is essential for the formation of hemoglobin of the blood, whose content depends to a large extent on one's state of health. An iron deficiency leads to anemia. The first symptom is a chronic feeling of fatigue. Athletes with an iron deficiency will not only feel fatigue, but will also notice such things as an unhealthy face coloring, headaches, shortness of breath (due to oxygen deficiency in the lungs), and increased irritability.

The assimilation of iron is a rather complex process. Sometimes the body doesn't assimilate even the best iron preparations. Iron assimilation is facilitated and greatly enhanced by vitamin C. Therefore, the combination of liver (which contains iron) with parsley (for vitamin C) is an excellent one.

Magnesium strengthens the teeth and prevents kidney stones. Magnesium is found in the seeds of the poppy plant, pumpkin, sunflowers, nuts, greens, and molasses. A very rich source of magnesium is cocoa. The absence of magnesium and vitamin B_6 in the body leads to quick weight gain, arteriosclerosis, and a real danger for the cardiovascular system. A deficiency of magnesium has as its initial symptoms a feeling of unease, fear, irritability, insomnia, and fatigue. Twitching of the eyelids is common.

Injuries and Their Prevention

The most vulnerable links of a judoka's support and movement apparatus are the knee, ankle, shoulder, and elbow joints. The spinal column is also vulnerable. The most frequent injuries are those of the meniscus of the knee joint and injuries to the side cruciate ligaments.

In a judoka's yearly training cycle the greatest number of injuries (around 70 percent) arise during periods of competition, which are the most intensive periods. Significantly fewer injuries (30 percent) occur during the training and transition periods. There are three times more injuries during workouts than during competition.

The main reasons for injuries are improper organization of the training process and competitions, errors in study methodology, competition rules violations, and technically incorrect application of a technique. Among organizational and methodological errors in a judoka's training process, special mention should be made of incorrect sparring matchups (disparity in weight categories and significant differences in skill levels and technical and physical preparedness), the introduction of game exercises in training under poor organizational and climatic conditions, flaws in equipment, judging, etc.

At the root of injuries in judo are, first of all, methodological flaws, including accelerated training, that is, abrupt increases in the scope and intensity of workouts.

At the beginning of a workout, injuries occur due to deficiencies in an athlete's psychological state and poor warm-up. At the end of a workout injuries occur as a result of fatigue. A large proportion (90 percent) of special training in the concluding stage of competition training deserves a coach's special attention, whereas special training (general developmental exercises and games) comprises only around 10 percent, which suggests, as in other sports, a certain narrowness of specialization.

Errors that lead to injuries are connected with game-type sports that are included in training without the requisite methodological, organizational, and technical support. In addition, they also stem from improper execution of special elements of an attack or defense. Injury causes for judoka is multifaceted. The direct cause of injury—falling and landing a strike—accounts for up to 40 percent of injuries; around 50 percent of injuries are caused by an abrupt, uncoordinated, or forceful bending, unbending, or twisting of a joint, and up to 10 percent are connected with a combination of injury-causing actions.

A violation in the execution of a technique leads to injury in both the offender and his rival (by a ratio of two to one). This situation may be explained by the psychic-emotional state of the judoka during training sessions, and knockout, elimination, and championship competitions. Studies show that judoka get injured because they are too relaxed or more often because they are too excited. Some injured judoka are known to be lacking a desire to fight or an extremely strong desire to win.

An athlete's psychic and emotional instability, a lack of the necessary level of moral and volitional preparation, and a lack of fighting qualities bear a relation not only to performance in athletic contests, but also, to a certain degree, to the frequency of injuries.

To prevent injuries it is important, first of all, to be strict in one's selection of partners. Pairs should form when both athletes are in the same weight category and are at the same level of technical preparedness. It is also essential to make sure that after a judoka has taken a break from classes he resume training with caution and with the permission of a physician.

One of the most important measures to prevent injuries in judo (as has already been noted) is to study methods of protection. The absence of cracks between mats, the integrity of the covering, and the presence of mats at the edges are elements that ensure safety.

When studying armlock and choke techniques, it is essential to make sure that the action be stopped immediately when the partner gives the surrender signal, either verbally or by slapping the mat or his partner.

On the next page is a table of approximate timeframes for resuming training and competition after injury. In each case, the decision should be made by a physician.

Table 6. Broken Bones

Injury	Number of Days	
	TRAINING Can Start	COMPETITION Is Possible
SHINS	80–90 from the day person regains mobility	110–120
FOREARMS	40–50 from the day person regains mobility	70–80
SHOULDERS	60–80 from the day person regains mobility	90–110
FEET	3–8 months after break	
RIBS	20–30 after break	46–60
COLLARBONE	40–60 after break	70–90
ANKLE SPRAINS		
First Degree	7–10	10–20
Second Degree	14–20	21–30
Third Degree	21–30	31–40
WRIST SPRAINS	7–20 from day of injury	
SHOULDER SPRAIN	90–130 days from day of injury	
KNEE SPRAINS AND INJURIES		
Without Hemartrosis	10–14 after injury	17–20
With Slight Hemorrhaging and Ligament Damage	14–28 after injury	4–35
With Pronounced Swelling and Ligament Damage	no sooner than 60 days after injury	
ELBOW AND SHOULDER		
Dislocation	30–60 after injury	90–150

First Aid

Unfortunately, as in any contact sport, especially one-on-one fighting, you can't get around injuries in judo classes. Regardless, only an expert with a medical degree can provide qualified assistance. Such experts should be present at all competitions. During training, the coach and athlete must know the rules and have the resources for providing aid before a doctor arrives.

Contusions

A contusion is damage to tissues and organs that occurs as a result of an action of short duration with some blunt object. These are the most common injuries encountered in judo classes. Contusions are closed wounds, since they do not involve breaking the body's outer covering.

In order to minimize the pain, stop hemorrhaging, and keep the swelling down after a contusion, the first thing to do is to apply cold to the injured area. This will constrict the blood vessels, decreasing the flow of blood to the injured area. For this you can use cold flowing water, a towel soaked in cold water, snow, if the injury occurs in winter, or a metallic object (weights from barbells and dumbbells that may be at the dojo).

Chlorotile is used in athletic practice. From a distance of 4 to 6 inches the injured area is sprayed from an ampoule until frost appears. It is better to smear the skin with a cream at first so as to avoid burning. Special gels (troxevasine, indovasine) have been shown to be effective.

A positive effect from the cold treatment is achieved from prolonged application (40 to 60 minutes per application, with breaks the first few days). Do not massage a newly injured area, apply heating ointments, or heat the area, because this leads to dilation of the blood vessels, increased blood flow, expansion of inter-tissue edema, and increased pain.

Bone Injuries

A dislocation is a displacement of the ends of bones united at a joint. Signs of a dislocation are a sharp pain in the joint when you try to move, swelling around the joint, inability to move at the joint, and a change in its form compared with the corresponding joint of the healthy end.

The first thing that must be done when a dislocation has occurred is to ensure that the injured extremity is completely relaxed. A dislocated arm must be suspended carefully, using a towel or belt or bandage. If a leg has become dislocated, lay the judoka down, putting something soft under his leg. Do not try to reset the dislocated joint, since a dislocation is frequently accompanied by a break, which can be set in a hospital or clinic.

A break is a more serious injury. There are closed breaks, in which the skin remains intact at the break site, and open ones, where there is an open wound at the break point.

Signs of a break include severe pain, swelling, and hemorrhaging around the break, a change in the shape of the broken extremity, movement of the skin at the break point, and an inability to move the extremity independently. The most important task in rendering first aid in the case of a break is to ensure that the broken bones remain completely immobile. For this, the broken extremity must be bandaged on a carrier veneer splint. You can use any long, even object as a splint.

In setting up the splint it is essential that:

1. The splint cover no fewer than two joints (above and below the break area) and extend significantly beyond the joints.
2. A soft material be placed between the splint and the extremity.
3. The splint be fastened firmly and evenly to the extremity with a bandage.

When setting up the splint on the arms, bend the arm at the elbow. For a leg injury, straighten the leg at the knee.

In case of a broken collarbone, it is essential to secure the arm so that it cannot move. In order to accomplish this, the arm should be bent at the elbow and suspended with a bandage (or belt). In addition, the shoulder should be fastened with a bandage to the upper body.

In case of broken ribs, the judoka is asked to take a deep breath and then exhale; at the moment of exhalation, his upper body is wrapped tightly with a wide bandage or towel.

Remember that qualified assistance can be rendered only by a physician. Thus, in the case of serious injury, it is essential to take the injured person to the hospital immediately.

Instead of a Conclusion

This book would not have been written if the authors, who have much competition and coaching experience and have done much research in judo, had not given serious attention to the study of the works of Russian physical education scholars and hadn't listened to the opinion of expert practitioners. We will not list all their names—the list of people is extraordinarily long and a failure to mention someone might be the cause of an unintended offense.

We dedicate this book to our coaches, friends, and rivals on the mat, judges, and health professionals—everyone who lives and breathes judo.

If you have never walked out on the mat, there is much you are missing out on. But it's not too late. Put on a judogi, tie your belt around your waist, and you're on your way. The incredible, mysterious, and open world of judo awaits you.

Glossary of Judo Techniques

Japanese Name of Technique	English Name of Technique
Ashi-Barai	Variation of Advancing Foot Sweep
Ashi-Gake	Leg Hook
Ashi-Garami	Entangled Leg Hook
Ashi-Gatame	Leg Armlock
Ashi-Guruma	Foot Wheel
Ashi-Uchi-Mata	Leg Inner Thigh Reaping Throw
Ashi-Jime	Leg Choke
De-Ashi-Barai	Advancing Foot Sweep
Do-Jime	Choke Technique: Executed by grabbing the torso with legs (banned in sport judo)
Ebi-Garami	Variation of Standing Choke Technique
Ebi-Jime	Standing Choke
Eri-Jime	Lapel Choke
Eri-Seoi-Nage	Lapel Shoulder Throw
Fumi-Komi-Seoi-Nage	Variation of Shoulder Throw
Gyaku-Gaeshi-Jime	Reverse Counter Choke Choke Technique: Tori is standing; uke is in front of him on all fours
Gyaku-Juji-Jime	Reverse Cross Strangle

Gyaku-Kataha-Jime	Reverse Single Wing Choke Choke Technique: Uke is on all fours; tori is standing in front of uke
Gyaku-Kesa-Garami	Reverse Scarf Lock
Gyaku-Kesa-Gatame	Reverse Scarf Hold
Gyaku-Okuri-Eri-Jime	Reverse Sliding Lapel Choke
Hadake-Jime	Naked Choke
Hane-Goshi	Springing Hip Throw
Hane-Maki-Komi	Outer Winding Spring Hip Throw
Hara-Gatame	Stomach Armlock
Harai-Goshi	Sweeping Hip Throw
Harai-Maki-Komi	Sweeping Hip Throw (variation in which, to complete the throw, tori throws his weight on uke as uke begins to fall)
Harai-Tsuri	Variation of Lifting Pulling Ankle Sweep
Harai-Tsuri-Komi-Ashi	Lifting Pulling Foot Sweep
Hasami-Jime	Scissors Choke with Opposite Lapel and Leg: Uke is on his stomach; tori is on his knees to the side
Hidari-Ashi-Jime	Left Leg Choke
Hidari-Kata-Seoi	Left Shoulder Throw
Hiji-Maki-Komi	Entangled Elbow
Hiji-Otoshi	Elbow Drop
Hikkomi-Gaeshi	Rolling Turn Over
Hiza-Gatame	Knee Armlock
Hiza-Guruma	Knee Wheel Throw
Hiza-Maki-Komi	Entangled Knee
Hon-Kesa-Gatame	Regular Scarf Lock
Ippon-Seoi-Nage	One-Arm Shoulder Throw
Jigoku-Jime	Hell Strangle
Juji-Gatame	Cross Armlock
Juji-Jime	Cross Choke
Kaeshi-Jime	Reverse Choke
Kagato-Jime	Double Foot Choke
Kami-Hiza-Gatame	Upper Knee Lock
Kami-Sankaku-Gatame	Upper Triangle Lock

Kami-Shiho-Gatame	Upper Four-Quarter Hold
Kami-Shiho-Jime	Upper Four-Quarter Choke
Kami-Ude-Hishigi-Juji-Gatame	Variation of Cross Armlock
Kani-Basami	Flying Scissors
Kannuki-Gatame	Armlock
Kashira-Gatame	Head Lock
Kata-Ashi-Dori	Single Leg Hold
Kata-Eri-Seoi-Nage	Lapel Shoulder Throw
Kata-Gatame	Shoulder Hold
Kata-Kesa-Gatame	Shoulder Scarf Hold
Kata-Guruma	Shoulder Wheel
Kata-Ha-Jime	Single Wing Strangle
Kata-Juji-Jime	Half Cross Strangle
Kata-Osae-Gatame	Shoulder Press Lock
Kata-Seoi	Single Shoulder Throw
Katate-Jime	One-Hand Choke
Katate-Seoi-Nage	One Hand Shoulder Throw
Ken-Ken-Uchi-Mata	Hopping Inner Thigh Reaping
Kesa-Garami	Scarf Entanglement
Kesa-Gatame	Scarf Hold
Ko-Soto-Barai	Minor Outer Sweep
Ko-Soto-Gake	Minor Outer Hook
Ko-Soto-Gari	Minor Outer Reaping
Ko-Tsuri-Goshi	Minor Lifting Hip Throw
Ko-Uchi-Barai	Minor Inner Sweep
Ko-Uchi-Gake	Minor Inner Hook
Ko-Uchi-Gari	Minor Inner Reaping
Ko-Uchi-Maki-Komi Minor	Inner Winding Throw
Koshi-Guruma	Hip Wheel Throw
Koshi-Uchi-Mata	Variation of Inner Thigh Reaping
Kubi-Nage	Neck Throw
Kibisu-Gaeshi	Heel Trip Reversal
Kuchiki-Taoshi	Pushing the Rotten Tree
Kuki-Nage	Air Throw
Kuzure-Kami-Shiho-Garami	Broken Upper Four-Quarter Entanglement

Kuzure-Kami-Shiho-Gatame	Broken Upper Four-Quarter Hold
Kuzure-Kesa-Gatame	Variation of Scarf Hold
Kuzure-Makura-Kesa-Gatame	Variation of Scarf Hold
Kuzure-Yoko-Shiho-Gatame	Broken Side-Locking Four-Quarter Hold
Kuzushi-Kesa-Gatame	Unbalancing Scarf Hold
Maki-Komi	Wraparound Throw
Maki-Komi-Seoi-Nage	Entangled Shoulder Throw
Maki-Tomoe	Wrapping Circle Throw
Makura-Kesa-Gatame	Pillow Hold (Variation of Scarf Hold)
Mochiage-Otoshi	Lifting Drop
Morote-Jime	Two-Arm Choke ("Whirligig")
Morote-Gari	Two-Hand Reaping
Morote-Seoi-Nage	Two-Arm Shoulder Throw
Morote-Seoi-Otoshi	Two-Arm Shoulder Drop
Mune-Gatame	Side-Locking Hold
Mune-Gyaku	Side Reversal
Nami-Juji-Jime	Normal Cross Strangle
Ni-Dan-Ko-Soto-Gari	Minor Double Outside Reap
Obi-Goshi	Belt Hip Throw
Obi-Otoshi	Belt-Lifting Drop
Obitori-Gaeshi	Belt-Grab Throw Counter
O-Goshi	Major Hip Throw
O-Guruma	Major Wheel
Okuri-Ashi-Barai	Sliding Foot Sweep
Okuri-Eri-Jime	Sliding Lapel Choke
O-Soto-Gari Major	Outer Reaping
O-Soto-Guruma	Major Outer Wheel
O-Soto-Maki-Komi	Major Outer Wraparound
O-Soto-Otoshi	Major Outer Drop
Othen-Jime	Choke Variation
Othen-Gatame	Choke Variation
O-Uchi-Barai	Major Inner Sweep
O-Uchi-Gake	Major Inner Hook
O-Uchi-Gari	Major Inner Reaping

O-Uchi-Mata	Variation of Inner Thigh Reaping
Ryo-Ashi-Dori	Two-Leg Throw
Ryote-Jime	Two-Hand Choke
Sankaku-Ude-Kansetsu	Triangle Armlock
Sangaku-Jime	Triangle Choke
Sasae-Tsuri-Komi-Ashi	Lifting Pulling Ankle Sweep
Seoi-Age	Shoulder Lift
Seoi-Maki-Komi	Shoulder Wraparound
Seoi-Nage	Shoulder Throw
Seoi-Otoshi	Shoulder Drop
Sode-Guruma	Sleeve Wheel
Sode-Tsuri-Komi-Goshi	Sleeve Lifting Pulling Hip Throw
Soto-Gake	Outer Hook
Soto-Maki-Komi	Outer Wraparound
Sukui-Nage	Scoop Throw
Sumi-Gaeshi	Corner Reversal
Sumi-Otoshi	Corner Drop
Tai-Otoshi	Body Drop
Tani-Otoshi	Valley Drop
Tate-Sankaku-Gatame	Variation of Vertical Four-Quarter Hold
Tate-Shiho-Gatame	Vertical Four-Quarter Hold
Taware-Gaeshi	Rice Bag Reversal
Te-Guruma	Hand Wheel
Tomoe-Jime	Circular Choke
Tomoe-Nage	Circle Throw
Tsubame-Gaeshi	Swallow Flight Reversal
Tsukikomi-Jime	Thrusting Choke
Tsuri-Goshi	Lifting Hip Throw
Tsuri-Komi-Ashi	Lifting Pulling Foot Sweep
Tsuri-Komi-Goshi	Lifting Pulling Hip Throw
Uchi-Mata	Inner Thigh Reaping Throw
Uchi-Mata-Maki-Komi	Inner Thigh Wraparound Throw
Uchi-Mata-Mari-Komi	Variation of Inner Thigh Reaping
Uchi-Mata-Sukashi	Inner Thigh Reaping Throw Side Slip
Ude-Garami	Entangled Armlock

Ude-Garami-Henkawaza	Changing Entangled Armlock
Ude-Gatame	Variation of Upper Arm Crush
Ude-Hishigi	Variation of Arm Crush
Ude-Hishigi-Hara-Gatame	Stomach Armlock
Ude-Hishigi-Henkawaza	Arm Crush
Ude-Hishigi-Hiza-Gatame	Arm Crush Knee Armlock
Ude-Hishigi-Juji-Gatame	Arm Crush Cross Armlock
Ude-Hishigi-Ude-Gatame	Arm Crush Arm Armlock
Ude-Hishigi-Waki-Gatame	Arm Crush Armpit Armlock
Uki-Gatame	Floating Hold
Uki-Goshi	Floating Hip Throw
Uki-Otoshi	Floating Drop
Uki-Waza	Floating Throw
Ura-Gatame	Back Hold
Ura-Juji-Jime	Back Single Cross Choke
Ura-Kami-Shiho-Gatame	Variation of Upper Hold
Ura-Nage	Back Throw
Ura-Shiho-Gatame	Shoulder Hold
Ushiro-Goshi	Rear Hip Throw
Ushiro-Jime	Rear Forearm Choke
Ushiro-Nage	Rear Throw
Ushiro-Kesa-Gatame	Reverse Scarf Hold
Ushiro-Yoko-Shiho-Gatame	Reverse Side Four-Quarter Hold
Utsuri-Goshi	Changing Hip Throw
Waki-Gatame	Armpit Hold
Yama-Arashi	Mountain Storm Throw
Yoko-Gake	Side Hook
Yoko-Guruma	Side Wheel
Yoko-Hiza-Gatame	Side Knee Hold
Yoko-Otoshi	Side Drop
Yoko-Shiho-Gatame	Side Four-Quarter Hold
Yoko-Tomoe	Side Circle
Yoko-Ude-Hishigi	Side Arm Crush
Yoko-Wakare	Side Separation